One Day In Alabama

Clarke Stallworth

Seacoast Publishing
Birmingham, Alabama

Published by Seacoast Publishing, Inc.
110 12th Street North
Birmingham, Alabama 35203

Cover art by Carol Middleton
Text art by Jodie Potter

ISBN 1-878561-37-5

To obtain copies of this book, please write or call:
Seacoast Publishing, Inc.
110 12th St. North
Birmingham, AL 35203
(205) 250-8016

Dedication

To my sisters—Mary King McCarroll, Margaret Carlton, Madelyn Thomas and Helen Burke Liles—who surrounded me with stories and believed in me as a writer. Also to my late parents, Mary Carter Adams Stallworth and Dr. Clarke J. Stallworth. Now and again they told me to leave the book in the front porch swing and go out to play, but they weren't really serious.

Table of Contents

Preface 7

Chapter 1—1817
Noblemen search for Utopia
In Alabama wilderness 15

Chapter 2—1818
Alabama capitol
"A place of bats and owls" 23

Chapter 3—1819
Dusty horseman in Huntsville?
"It's President Monroe!" 31

Chapter 4—1820
A horse stumbles in the forest,
And Alabama history changes direction 37

Chapter 5—1825
Hail the Hero!
LaFayette visits Alabama 43

Chapter 6—1831
Hero of the Alamo
On run the from Alabama 49

Chapter 7—1832
GOLD IN ALABAMA! blared the newspaper,
And gold rush was on 55

Chapter 8—1832
An Alabama belle tamed Sam Houston,
Hero of San Jacinto 61

Chapter 9—1833
Star Spangled Banner author
Kept Alabama out of rebellion 67

Chapter 10—1834
Students shoot
At University president 73

Chapter 11—1835
Menawa touches land one last time,
Then walks Trail of Tears 81
Chapter 12—1836
A tearful farewell to Alabama
From an Indian named Eufaula 91
Chapter 13—1846
"Government on wheels"
Settles on Goat Hill 99
Chapter 14—1854
For a moment in history,
Steamboat is king of Alabama's rivers 107
Chapter 15—1854
Archaelaus spoke,
And two colleges were born 115
Chapter 16—1858
Love and death
On the flaming river 123
Chapter 17—1861
Alabama militia capture forts
Before Civil War begins... 133
About the author 141

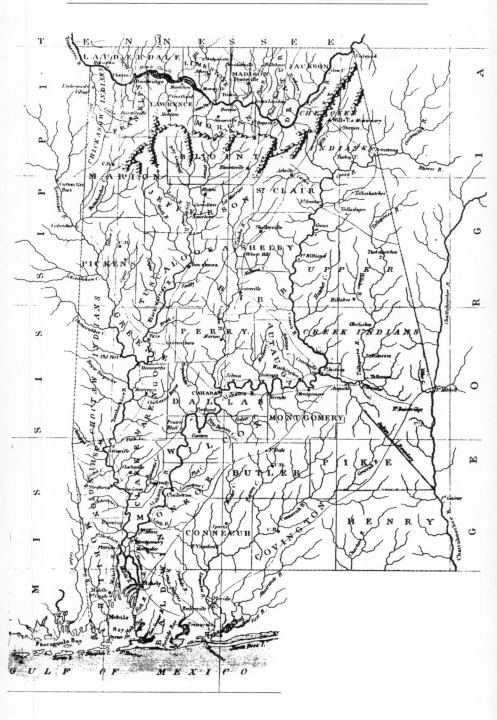

The South is stories

When I was growing up a doctor's son in Marengo County, the history of my state trickled down to me from textbooks as a collection of old men with beards and high collars, a gray tapestry of dull events interwoven with meaningless dates.

I carried this lifeless vision into manhood.

In the middle 1970s, I was city editor of *The Birmingham News*, a reasonably successful journalist who had abandoned writing for the higher pay and questionable prestige of an editor's job.

But there was something missing from my life. At base, I was a writer, and I was not writing. I was reading copy, lots of copy, from obits to features to hard news stories, but my fingers itched for the keyboard.

I had grown up reading books in a green front porch swing in Thomaston, Alabama, and I had always wanted to put those words on the page.

But now, with my brain eternally playing catch-up with too much copy and not enough help on the desk, what would I write? I looked around for some subject which hadn't been spoken for. I couldn't just go out and poach on somebody else's beat.

So I created my own beat, a new one. An idea bubbled to the top of my mind: How about the stories out of Alabama history? Nobody had staked out that claim, and Alabama history could not possibly be as dull as the history textbooks made out.

The idea crystallized into a plan. I would find the facts and write them, in narrative style, as stories, and maybe I could make them interesting to newspaper readers.

I took an afternoon off from the obits and the telephone calls of the city desk, and went over to the Birmingham Public Library. Mary Bess Kirksey and her friends in the Southern History Room thought I had a good idea.

They pitched in to help: Mary Bess, Tom Miller, Yvonne Crumpler, Ann Tyler and later, Jennie Kimbrough Scott and Anne Knight.

They dug out books, marked the interesting places, and had them piled on the table when I got to the fourth floor. They looked up facts for me, they remembered their own favorite stories out of Alabama's past. They thought history was alive, and fun.

So I bent over the books in the library, burrowed beneath the surface of Alabama history, and found a treasure — jeweled stories glittering in the fluorescent library light.

There, just beneath the gray surface, were the people. Fighting, living, loving, rescuing each other, robbing each other, killing each other. Heroes, hero-ines, outlaws, bastards, saints, greedy people, pitiful people, mean people, weak people and people with wills like iron rods.

And their stories. Oh, their stories. The truth,

better than the novels I had read in that front porch swing on that Thomaston front porch. Great things, shameful things, fascinating things, human things, ranging up and down the warp and woof of Alabama history like a golden thread.

So, in *The Birmingham News* on Sundays, I began to write stories out of Alabama history. I called it "A Day in the Life of Alabama." Some were all right, some were downright dull, and some of them were pretty good. I look at some of them now, and get that writer's tingle: Hey, I wrote that.

I took some license with the stories. I bridged some gaps with my imagination. I did my homework, and the stories are historically accurate.

Ray Brown and Benny Yates of *The News* illustrated the stories, and their pictures made the stories come alive.

People read them. Teachers clipped them, and used them to help teach Alabama history to children. Maybe they helped some kid to know that Alabama history was alive, not dead.

Now and then, somebody would stop me on my way up 20th Street to the YMCA at lunchtime, and tell me he liked the story last Sunday about the Confederate spy, or the pioneer woman. I liked that.

The message began to filter back to me: Other people were fed up with the idea of Alabama history as a collection of colorless, bloodless, cardboard figures. They were hungry for stories too.

The stories seemed to give people a better handle on their place. To know who did what, 200 years ago or 25 years ago, seemed to help them understand themselves better.

To me, it was more than that. It was like pulling a gauzy veil, a curtain, back from a stage. Once I had seen dull gray figures standing stiffly, motionless, on that stage of history.

Now, with the curtain pulled back, I saw living,

breathing, fighting, bleeding, loving, hating, working, people. To me, each story I wrote added another character to my stage.

I remember going on a midshipman cruise on a destroyer out of Newport, Rhode Island, in the late 1940s, when I was in the Naval ROTC program at Chapel Hill. On the destroyer were students from the great Ivy League universities.

Alabama was something to be ashamed of — first in poverty, last in education; first in hookworm and pellagra, last in literacy; first in hickdom and redneckery, last in culture. And if we escaped the bottom rung in any category, thank God for Mississippi.

And besides, we had lost the war. Glorious in defeat, certainly, shades of knights of old in a Walter Scott novel, and the keening, indomitable sound of a Rebel yell coming from that ragged gray line, moving across the meadow. But we had lost.

That was one thing the old Alabama history textbooks did well. They made defeat seem like victory, somehow.

At North Carolina, I had dreams of playing Edward R. Murrow, talking with a deep authoritative voice into New York microphones. I talked endlessly into a recorder, sitting in the attic of the SAE house, trying to strip away the levels of my Southern accent. I learned to say "North CArolina" instead of "Nawth CahLIna."

And that, to me now, is somehow sad.

All the Southern stereotypes on radio and television were fools, thick accents dripping with ignorance. I didn't want to be a Senator Claghorn, suh, so I learned to say "North CArolina."

Since then, I have come full circle. With the rich images of my Alabama stories in my head, I have become a Southern — and an Alabama — chauvinist.

We are not only as good as people from other regions of America, we are better. And it is not football that makes it so.

We Southerners, thank God, are distinctive. We are different. Our stories, our land, our heritage, make us different. Southerners, and especially Alabamians, are lucky. We are simply more interesting than people who live in other places. Our stories make it so.

Don't misunderstand me. I know we have large problems in Alabama and the South. I know we are defensive, prickly, too quick to raise our fists. I know our schools are not high quality.

We need more high tech skills, we need more intelligent diversification of our industries, we need a better-educated workforce. We need to splice higher education and research together, our ticket into the future. We need tax reform, so that the greedy timber and pulp companies pay their fair share of property tax, and channel more tax money into our starving schools.

We have many needs, no doubt about that. We are always playing catch up with the rest of the nation. But there is a bright side, even to that dark coin.

In the South, we are late bloomers, thank God. We were held back, and the calculated economic punishment after the Civil War has turned into a blessing.

If we were held back, by discriminatory freight rates or the patronizing sneers of the Eastern money, our luck was holding.

So far, we have escaped the layers of sterile grayness they call progress in some places. We have not, as yet, sold our birthright for a mess of technological porridge. I hear they have a great porridge restaurant in Atlanta, just off Peachtree.

By starting late, we still have a chance to make technology serve us, do what we want it to do. We have a chance to join enlightened technology with our rich heritage, and create a humane life worth living.

But our heritage is at the core of it all. Without it, we will become the pasteurized, homogenized, tasteless, bloodless robots of the future, bland prisoners of technology.

And our heritage—this talisman of the modern South—flows to us from our stories.

In Alabama and the South, we still have the problems of race—to find the combination which will allow black and white people to live together peacefully. But Alabamians—black and white—surely will reach an accommodation long before the people of the clogged cities of the North, because we share stories and the land and our heritage.

The only way we can come to maturity as a state, as a people, is to know ourselves—where we are, what we are, who we are. If we position ourselves between our past and our future, we can walk forward with knowledge and confidence and pride. And we can be happy doing it.

But we can only position ourselves—find out who and where and what we are—by knowing our past, by knowing our stories. We don't have to agree with all the things in our heritage, but we must know about them, and accept them.

To me, stories are magic. They helped me to find myself as a writer, to know where I am and who I am. And there is a lot of joy, both in listening to stories and in telling them.

My friend, come closer to the fire, let me tell you about some people, in a place called Alabama.

****

Summer, 1995, a postscript:

It was fun, watching my little book spread its wings and fly. Not very high, and not very far yet, but it's flying, it's off the ground. And that's a pleasure. I have had fun with it, reading stories to fourth graders, and watching their eyes light up at a good story out of Alabama history. I like for strangers to come up to me and tell me they like my book, that they had no idea Alabama history was so interesting. I believe I'm on the right track, and here is the second installment of stories in the series. If I can get you interested in your past, if I can help you position yourself between the past and the future, if I can help you find out who you are, I can make a difference.

Chapter One

1817

————

Noblemen search For Utopia in Alabama wilderness

Some of the Choctaws came out of the woods to look.

It was a strange sight. There was the muddy river down below, with alligators sunning themselves on the banks, and the thick woods stretching from either side.

And, in the midst of the Alabama wilderness of 1817, on a cleared-out flat place at the top of the white bluffs above the river, the white people were dancing.

The women wore jewels and bright ball gowns, their hems raising little puffs of white dust as they swirled to the music of the violins, and some of the men wore jeweled swords and bright sashes, the residue of Napoleon's grand army.

The Indians watched, and shook their heads, and melted back into the woods.

It was the spring of 1817, and the place was Demopolis, near the confluence of the Warrior and Tombigbee Rivers, in the Mississippi Territory. It would be two years before Alabama became a state.

While Napoleon was riding high—either the scourge or the savior of Europe, depending on your point of view—the dancers on the white bluff had been the flower of French society—officers, architects, scholars, and their cultured, perfumed ladies.

When Napoleon fell at Waterloo, and the English packed him off to St. Helena and exile, his leaders were exiled too. Some of them sailed to America, and in the fall of 1816 the French Immigration Association was formed in Philadelphia.

The émigrés had visions of a great new community they would found in America—a Utopian place where they grow grapes (for wine) and olives. It would be a place of high civilization, where the highest of the Napoleonic era would exist side by side with good honest work.

Leader of the émigrés was Gen. Count Charles Lefebvre Desnouettes, who had shared a sleigh with Napoleon on the bloody retreat from Moscow in the snow.

When Napoleon bid good-bye to his troops, he put his arms around Desnouettes and said: "I shall embrace Gen. Desnouettes on behalf of you all."

The émigrés sent out searching parties for just the right place to build their Utopia. Some went to Ohio. Another party went to Kentucky, and there were told of a place in the Mississippi Territory, a place where two rivers came together.

On March 6, 1817, the U.S. Congress gave the French émigrés a grant on the Tombigbee River—four townships, a total of 144 square miles, at a price of $2 an acres, with 14 years to pay.

In April of 1817, the schooner *McDonough* unfurled its sails out of the harbor in Philadelphia, and pointed its bow to the south, heading around Florida. The French ladies stood at the rail, dressed in their Parisian finery. They had a few vine and olive plants, and a few farm implements.

They rounded Florida, sailed to the north in the Gulf of Mexico, but ran into rough weather off Mobile Point. The ship went aground, then came off, and sailed into Mobile. After hospitality and parties, the party sailed up towards the Tombigbee on a revenue cutter.

At St. Stephens, they left the cutter and began the laborious voyage up the Tombigbee on rafts. On the banks of the river they saw deer and other wild animals—bears and panthers—and Indians, peering out from behind the trees.

At last they reached the chalky bluffs just below the confluence of the Warrior and the Tombigbee.

They pulled their rough craft out onto the bank and said: Here will be our city, Demopolis, the city of the people.

They unloaded and bravely struck out into the woods to cut trees and build log cabins.

They cleared a level place on the bluff over the river, dusted off their ball gowns and sashed uniforms, and had a stately dance of celebration.

They named the county Marengo (after Napoleon's battle with the Austrians on June 4, 1800), and the county seat, today called Linden, after the village of Hohenlinden, site of another battle on Dec. 3, 1800.

But high ideals and civilized conversation and bright red sashes did not a colony make.

They had settled in a place of fertile Canebrake soil, later called the Black Belt for the black earth. But it was better suited for cotton than for grapes and olives. Ironically, there was an ideal place for vines and olives about 30 miles to the north.

They had no wagons, their wells went dry, the river overflowed into their fields, mosquitoes brought malaria and the yellow shakes. They chose the most beautiful sites for their homes, but sadly the prettiest places sometimes seemed to have the poorest land. Nothing seemed to go right.

The émigrés refused to use slaves—*Liberte, egalite, fraternite!*—but they did import some German redemptioners who worked out their passage. And the Choctaws helped, coming out of the woods to show them how to grow food.

Like the tolling of a bell, hardship followed hardship, misfortune trailed misfortune, but they kept their gay spirits. After felling logs and clearing fields, there were court balls in rough-hewn log cabins, wine drunk from exquisite cut glass goblets, food eaten with silver forks.

General Desnouettes built a sanctuary, a small cabin with a bust of Napoleon sitting in the place of honor. Inside there were flags, standards, swords, pistols, things to remind him of glories past.

A year after they settled at Demopolis, disaster struck like a lightning bolt. They learned they had misread their maps and settled in the wrong place. Their grant—land granted from the U.S. Congress—was farther to the east.

Sadly, the émigrés packed up their goblets, their books, their china, their silver, and their red sashes, and walked away from the cabins they had built and the land they had cleared.

They resettled in a place they called Aigleville (Eagleville, in honor of the eagles on the standards of Napoleon.)

Again, the backbreaking toil of clearing ground, cutting trees, fitting the logs into cabins, building another life.

The convivial French, loving their own company and their social life, built their cabins in clusters, far from their fields. They would have done better to scatter their homes out among the individual farms, but they liked to be together.

So they had to pay the price—they lived miles from farms, in some cases, and they had to make long trips each day, miles from home to farm, then more miles back home.

Soon they saw their mistakes, and moved again, this time farther east, closer to their farms, to a place they called Arcola, after a battle fought with the Austrians, in November of 1796.

The parade of troubles continued. Some of their olive trees were killed by frost, and the grapes matured too early to make the kind of wines they wanted. The year of 1818 was "eighteen hundred and starve to death," according to some of the colonists.

In 1827, a hard frost killed the grape vines to the roots, and the vine and olive colony began to unravel.

Some of the colonists went back to Mobile, where the niceties of French life could be observed. Some went back to Philadelphia, and some even went back to France. Some stayed in Marengo County and built up profitable plantations—using slaves to grow cotton.

Desnouettes wrote his wife in France: He was leaving, he could take it no longer. His wife, a sister of the banker Lafitte, was a rich women, and spent a fortune supporting the general and his colony.

Dogged with hard luck to the last, Desnouettes boarded a ship bound for Belgium and reunion with his wife. The ship was wrecked off Ireland, and the general went down with the ship.

There is a tragedy contained in the story of Alabama's Vine and Olive Colony.

It is a story of contrasts, of elements like water and oil, which would not mix.

To make it on the frontier, you had to be strong, and you had to be tough. And you had to be willing to spend much of your life alone.

You had to be satisfied with simple pleasures, and you had to obey the first last of the frontier: Thou shalt be frugal, or thou shalt starve.

The émigrés, in their magnificent ignorance of frontier life, thought they could have it all—fruitful crops and leisure, rich plantations and time for dancing and civilized conversation.

And they stuck with a pre-conceived idea—they would grow grapes and olives, no matter what, even when the land was made for cotton.

They could not, would not, change, and their inability to change brought them to the year of "eighteen hundred and starve to death."

To make it on the frontier, you had to be strong, and you had to be tough. And you had to be willing to spend much of your life alone.

Chapter Two

1818

Alabama capital "A place of Bats and owls"

Around their campfires, the Choctaw Indian children shivered to hear the bloody legend of the place called Hobuckintopa.

It was a white bluff overlooking the river, limestone cliffs stretching above the muddy Tombigbee in what is now Washington County. Indians avoided the place, walking miles out of the way to get around it, remembering the legend. To them, Hobuckintopa was a place of death.

An English army officer, Capt. Bernard Romans stood there, one day in the winter of 1772, on the flat plain overlooking the white limestone cliff, and he watched the river change personality.

Upstream, the Tombigbee River was frowning and treacherous, flexing its watery muscle against the rocks. Romans and his exploring party had come down the river, weaving their canoes among the white water, swerving to avoid the foaming rocks, and across the cresting water of the sandbars.

Downstream from St. Stephens, the river broke into a smile. The muddy river ran serene and deep on its way to Mobile and the Gulf of Mexico. Romans saw that the river, after exhausting itself on the last rapid, the final rocks, would be navigable all the way up from Mobile.

Romans had been sent exploring by his British superiors in Mobile. He and his party of friendly Indians had gone overland up into Mississippi, all the way past the present site of Columbus, and had curved back south on the Tombigbee River in their dugout canoes.

They had fought the river, and now, at the haunted bluff called Hobuckintopa, the struggle was over. From here to Mobile, the dugouts would move peacefully downstream. Romans knew what he had found, as he looked down the white bluff.

"Stout sloops and schooners may come up to this rapid; therefore I judge some considerable settlements will take place here," he wrote.

Romans was right. A "considerable settlement" did take place at the haunted bluff, as the Indians shook their heads. It was jinxed, they said. It was not a fit place for humans, it was haunted. Sooner or later, the place would be inhabited only by bats and owls.

The white people laughed, and built their houses.

In 1780, as the Americans stood on the edge of independence from England, Spanish troops pushed the English out of Mobile and moved up Alabama's rivers, hungry for territory and gold.

The Spanish saw the looming white bluff, and the rapids, and listened to the Choctaw legend—a mutilated Indian warrior who threw himself off the bluff into the river. The Spanish nodded, paying no heed to the Indian nonsense, and built their fort at the first rapids.

The soldiers cut trees, and stacked them into a fort and called it St. Stephens, and their cannon controlled the river below.

As the years passed, American settlers trickled into the area from Georgia and South Carolina and Tennessee. They looked at the Spanish fort, and called for a survey. They thought St. Stephens should lie in American—not Spanish—territory.

The survey was made in 1799, dividing the territory between the U.S. and Spain. The line was drawn south of St. Stephens, and the Spanish soldiers reluctantly shouldered their muskets and marched down to their boats, heading South, back to their port of Mobile.

St. Stephens became a flourishing frontier town, with homes, stores, an Indian trading post, and traders even extended credit to the Indians as they bought cloth and iron tools.

But the settlers of St. Stephens still were unhappy. They were part of the U.S., sure, part of the Mississippi Territory (which contained the states of Mississippi and Alabama). But the capital of the territory, near Natchez, was hundreds of miles away.

The Indians were unruly, occasionally attacking settlers, and the Mississippi government didn't keep enough soldiers in Alabama to control them.

And below them, the Spaniards held Mobile, and taxed the settlers on everything that came through the port city. The Spanish taxed them on goods they shipped out of Mobile, and they taxed them on the goods brought into Mobile.

They're taxing us coming and going, grumbled the settlers.

It was frustrating. The Indians were increasingly unfriendly, the Spanish in Mobile bled them white with high taxes coming and going, and the Natchez government didn't seem to care about them at all.

In 1809, the settlers met in Washington County, and vented their frustrations in a petition to the U.S. Congress. They complained of the Indians and Spaniards, and said the government in Mississippi could not look out for them "whilst the chief magistrate is remote from us, and a stranger to our sorrows and our sufferings."

With the taxes they had to pay the Spanish in Mobile, "we often pay for the flour of Kentucky and Pennsylvania four times the price that is paid by our fellow citizens of Natchez.

But Congress did nothing. It received the petition, and sat on it, put it in a pigeonhole and forgot about it. In 1813, the Americans took Mobile from Spain, and this burr was finally plucked from beneath the saddle of the settlers.

Through the early years of the new century, the Alabamians fought for separation from Mississippi.

The War of 1812 came, the Creek Wars ravaged the countryside, and still Congress would not move on Alabama's bid for statehood.

Finally, with the help of some friendly Georgians in Congress, on March 3, 1817, Congress cut the Mississippi Territory in half—creating the state of Mississippi and the Territory of Alabama. Half a loaf, but better than no bread at all.

Mississippi and Alabama haggled over the boundary line. Mississippi wanted Mobile, but the Alabamians, remembering the grudging taxes paid to the Spaniards, pointed to the Alabama river system that came together at Mobile, and would not yield.

Mobile is ours, they pounded on the desk. And the Alabamians won—Mobile remained part of Alabama.

President James Monroe sent a territorial governor, Dr. William Wyatt Bibb of Georgia.

And, with some solemnity, the Legislature of the Territory of Alabama came and to order and convened in St. Stephens on Jan. 19, 1818—in two rooms of the Douglass Hotel.

At this time, St. Stephens was a city of 40 houses, stores, taverns and other business establishments. There was a landing, a cleared place where boats could pull up on shore, at the foot of the bluff. There were two hotels, the Douglass and one run by the Alstons.

The streets were paved with brick or stone, and horses clopped along them on the way to the public square. Actors trod the boards of a prospering theater, and glasses were raised in several taverns.

There were no churches—religion was not welcome in the rawhide tough frontier. Some called St. Stephens a "churchless and godless place, with a prevailing indifference to anything that savored of religion."

In the two rooms of the Douglass Hotel, the territorial Legislature was gaveled to order for its first meeting. Gabriel Moore was elected Speaker of the House of Representatives, and James Titus of Madison County was elected head of the Council, comparable to the Alabama Senate of today.

Titus, in fact, was the only member of the Council. In some of the rooms of the Douglass, Titus gravely called himself to order, made motions, seconded his own motions, and solemnly voted for them, then recorded the vote. It was always 1-0, one way or the other.

The 12 members of the Assembly (the House of Representatives) met in another room.

The new governor, Bibb, had just resigned from the U.S. Senate as a senator from Georgia. He had voted for a congressional pay raise, in effect raising his own pay, and the voters in Georgia raised so much cain about it that he was forced out of office.

The Legislature established some new counties,

chartered a state bank, incorporated a steamboat company (the first steamboat built in Alabama was finished there later in 1818), chartered an academy at St.
Stephens, and repealed the law fixing a maximum
interest rate.

The Legislature also granted Alabama's first di-
vorce (Elizabeth Bennett divorced James Bennett) and
the first slave manumission (a free Negro of Mobile,
Honore Colin, freed his female slave, Rozetta).

The Legislature voted to make Huntsville the
temporary capital and Cahaba, on the Alabama River
below Selma, the permanent capital.

The next year, in 1819, the eager Alabamians left
their territorial status and achieved their ambition—
full statehood. And the government packed up its
records and moved to Huntsville, to wait for Cahaba,
the new capital city to be built in Dallas County.

And St. Stephens, which had been an extension of
the Natchez government in the territorial days, began
to shrivel when its umbilical cord to Natchez was cut.

There was a yellow fever epidemic in St. Stephens,
and the gravediggers were busy. There were empty
houses, and during the 1830s, St. Stephens ceased to
exist as a town. By 1860, the streets were empty, and
the dire Choctaw prediction came true—it was a place
of bats and owls.

An early Washington County historian recalled
waiting for a steamboat on the bank of the Tombigbee
near St. Stephens. He remembered "talking with some
hunters who had come with some wild turkeys killed on
the deserted streets of old St. Stephens."

Today, even the great white bluff of Hobuckintopa
is gone. It was quarried for limestone to make cement,
and automobile tires now hum across the concrete
highways of the state, across bits and pieces of Alabama history.

Go to St. Stephens today, and it is hard to find.
Cross a barbed-wire fence, walk along a logging road,

and finally, among the blackberry bushes and the scrub pine, you may find some crumbled bricks, or a gravestone, sunken halfway into the ground. Or a stone marker, lonely among the leaves.

St. Stephens, the haunted Hobuckintopa, the place where Alabama was born, is gone.

President Monroe

Chapter Three

1819

Dusty horseman In Huntsville? 'It's President Monroe!'

The three horsemen pulled up at the edge of the small Alabama town on the Tennessee River, and the spare-faced man wiped his forehead with a handkerchief.

One of the other riders asked a passing carpenter about an inn, and the man pointed with his hammer down the dusty street.

The horsemen clopped on down the street, and the carpenter stood there, holding his hammer, watching them. He suddenly broke into a run, heading for the nearest store, a clapboard building with a high false front.

"It's the President," he panted to the men at the counter inside, "That's President Monroe just rode into town."

The crowd gathered in front of the Green Bottom Inn, one of the best hotels in town. One of Huntsville's prominent citizens, Clement C. Clay Sr., spruced himself up and went inside to talk to the spare-faced man. Sure enough, it was President James Monroe, a long way from Washington, D.C.

Clay cleared his throat and said, in an official voice: *We had no idea you were coming, Mr. President. If we had known...*

President Monroe held up his hand. *No need for a big welcoming committee, I'm just making a turn through the country, examining the ground for possible fortifications in case we are attacked by an aggressor.*

Monroe and his companions—a private secretary named Governeur and an Army lieutenant named Monroe, no kin—had ridden to Huntsville from Augusta, Ga.

Later, they would move on up to Nashville, Tenn., Louisville and Lexington, Ky., before heading over the mountains back to Washington.

Monroe's story about "looking for sites for possible fortifications" may have been true, but it was not the complete truth by any means. Monroe and the speaker of the U.S. House of Representatives—Henry Clay of Kentucky—were fighting it out over something called "The American System."

Clay espoused "The American System," which proposed to push the U.S. westward with construction of new roads and canals, and to enact a protective tariff to stop foreign imports and encourage manufacturing in the North.

Monroe balked at the plan, doubting whether the federal government had the power to build roads and canals. But, as the pressure from Congress mounted, Monroe shrugged his shoulders: *Well, I'll just go and have a look, that's the best way to find out if roads and canals are needed.*

So he and his two companions took off for a swing through the Southeast—on horseback, moving slowly down the primitive trails. Through Indian country, from village to village, the President clopped along, talking to people, looking at transportation conditions—roads and rivers—along the way.

And, on June 1, 1819, he and his companions swung into Huntsville, the village where Hunt's Spring bubbled from the ground. Now it was Alabama's capital city, the temporary capital while the new capital city—Cahaba on the Alabama River—was being built.

As Clement Clay looked at Monroe, he may have thought of the resemblance Monroe had to George Washington—tall, rawboned, straight-backed from military service, gray-blue eyes inspiring confidence.

We must have a dinner for you, Mr. President, insisted Clay, and Monroe shrugged his approval.

The dinner was laid out in what was known as the Assembly Hall, an old frame building which stood at the southwest corner of the intersection of Franklin and Gates streets. The guest list was pared down to 100, after some discussion and much back-biting.

The local newspaper, *The Republican*, had this to say:

"On Wednesday at four o'clock, the President and suite, together with more than 100 of the most respectable citizens of Madison County, sat down to a sumptuous entertainment prepared by Capt. Toby Jones, at which Col. Leroy Pope acted as president, assisted by C. C. Clay and Henry Minor, Esq., as the following sentiments were drunk, accompanied by the discharge of cannon, and appropriate songs."

Glasses were raised, and drained, and raised again. A total of 21 assigned toasts were drunk, ranging from "Our Country" to "The Memory of Washington" to "Our Fair Countrywomen" to "Agriculture, Commerce and Manufacture."

Between the toasts, there was the boom of cannon from outside the assembly hall, and the voices raised in patriotic song.

One toast, addressed to "Our Distinguished Guest," went something like this: "We rejoice that he lives to dispense the blessings which flow from the achievements in which he participated. His country will never forget the man whose life has been so successfully devoted to her service." It was possible that someone had stayed up late the night before, working on that one.

The President arose, and returned thanks to the group for this kind expression. Later, the company broke into applause as he expressed the hope that Alabama's speedy admission into the Union might advance her happiness and augment the national strength and prosperity. (Alabama did become a state later that same year, with Monroe's blessing.)

Accounts of the visit say that the company rose from the table after sunset "highly delighted with the entertainment they had received and the opportunity they had enjoyed of demonstrating their great regard and affection for Mr. Monroe."

To one observer, the President appeared "more like a plain citizen than the Chief Magistrate of a great nation." Apparently, his unostentatious manners endeared him to everyone there.

Next day, June 3, 1819, Monroe and his two companions mounted their horses and headed north toward Nashville. He was "escorted by a number of respectable citizens several miles on his way," according to the newspaper report.

There were three horsemen, with a gaggle of towns-people trailing behind. One man pulled up alongside the President, and they talked and laughed. Then the man pulled up, to allow one of his neighbors a chance to talk to the President

Finally, the townspeople reined in their horses, and the President waved good-bye to them. One report says they parted "with most cordial expressions of good will."

On to Nashville, Louisville and Lexington. More dinners. More inspection. And back to Washington by July 15.

The fight with Henry Clay continued. In 1822, Monroe vetoed a bill providing for federal administration of toll gates on the Cumberland Road. He urged a constitutional amendment to give Congress the power to promote internal improvements. And in 1824, Monroe signed the Survey Act, which planned improvements in the future.

Inevitably, the energy of the Americans won out, and they pushed westward with roads and canals, even though President Monroe shook his head.

Back in Alabama, Clement Clay became governor, serving during the Creek War of 1835 and 1836.

For the people of Huntsville, it would be a long time before they forgot the spectacle of President James Monroe, unannounced and dusty, riding into town on a horse.

Gov. Thomas Bibb

Gov. William Wyatt Bibb

Chapter Four

1820

A horse stumbles
In the forest,
And Alabama history
Changes direction

The big horse picked his way through the trees of the Autauga County forest, down the old Indian trail, that July day of 1820.

The man sat the horse well, erect yet relaxed, guiding the horse with a lean of the slight body and just a touch of the reins.

Suddenly the big horse snorted and stumbled,

falling heavily to the ground. The man, caught beneath him, uttered a sharp cry of pain. The horse struggled to get up, scrabbling his feet on the ground, and he stepped on the man. Another cry of pain.

As the horse trotted off in the direction of the house, the man lay there on the ground, alone on the Indian trail, holding his side and panting.

Soon there was a mixed clatter of hooves, and several horsemen swung out of their saddles, lifting the man's head. They carried him back to the house on a litter.

William Wyatt Bibb, first governor of Alabama, never recovered from the fall. He died a few days later at his Autauga County plantation.

His death brought a festering political rivalry— between the "Georgia faction" of South Alabama and the "North Carolina faction" of North Alabama—to a head. The fight set the political pattern in Alabama for generations.

In his short life—he was only 40 when he died— William Wyatt Bibb was a political meteor. Born in Virginia, he moved with his family to Georgia. His father, Capt. William Bibb, died in 1796, leaving a widow and eight children. Though financially strapped, Mrs. Bibb managed to send her eldest son to college.

William Wyatt Bibb attended William and Mary College and later the medical college of the University of Pennsylvania, where he received his M.D. in 1801.

Dr. Bibb set up his medical practice in Petersburg, Ga., but politics was a virus in his blood.

At age 21 he was elected to the Georgia House of Representatives and later to the Georgia Senate. He was elected to the U.S. House of Representatives in 1806, serving there until 1813. Then he was appointed to the U.S. Senate, but lost a bid for re-election in 1816.

In the Congress, he formed a fast friendship with President James Monroe, another Virginian. In April of 1817, after Bibb had been defeated in Georgia for re-election to the U.S. Senate, President Monroe found a job for his friend.

He appointed Bibb governor of the newly-formed Territory of Alabama. Within days, Bibb was participating in the territorial government at St. Stephens, on the lower Tombigbee.

Bibb's message to the territorial Legislature urged the formation of new schools and development of transportation, mainly the waterways.

In 1818, the territorial Legislature asked the U.S. Congress to let Alabama become a state instead of a territory. The legislators also selected, at Bibb's direction, a tract of land where the Cahaba River runs into the Alabama River, in Dallas County. It would be the new permanent state capital.

Bibb was commissioned to "lay off the town of Cahaba on this site."

Then, on July 9, the Alabama Constitutional Convention met in Huntsville to draft a constitution for the new state.

In the first gubernatorial election, Bibb ran against Marmaduke Williams of Tuscaloosa, a former congressman from North Carolina.

It was the beginning of the "Georgia vs. North Carolina" fight in Alabama politics. Bibb led the "Georgia faction," an aristocratic group mostly from South Alabama. They were rich; many of them had plantations and slaves, and they lived mostly along the banks of the Alabama River.

The "North Carolina" faction were mostly people who had been born in North Carolina and had trekked across the mountains into Tennessee, and from there down into Alabama. They lived mostly along the banks of the Tennessee River, as it dipped from Tennessee into Alabama and looped back again into Tennessee.

There were 15,482 votes cast in the statewide election, and Bibb squeaked to victory by 1,202 votes.

The Georgia people wanted representation in the

Legislature to be same for each county. But the North Carolina people wanted representation by population. More people lived in North Alabama than in South Alabama.

A compromise was struck, as it had been struck in 1787, at Philadelphia, in the U.S. Constitution. They would have representation by population, at least in the House, and each county would have a senator.

But the Georgia faction won a crucial victory: The permanent capital would be in Cahaba, in South Alabama, in "Georgia faction" territory.

It would be easier—the capital was closer—for the South Alabama legislators to get to the Legislature, and it meant that the North Alabama representatives would be absent more often. And this would give South Alabama an edge in votes. They thought of everything.

So the Georgia faction—representing mostly the educated, the rich and influential people of the state—took control of the state at first. They had the governor, and they had the capital close to home, which translated into more votes and control.

Then, on that day in July, a horse stumbled in the woods of Autauga County, and the river of Alabama politics took another turn.

Thomas Bibb, brother of William Wyatt Bibb, was president of the Alabama Senate and became governor on his brother's death.

William Wyatt Bibb had served less than a year, and Thomas Bibb served the remaining year and a half of the term.

But Thomas Bibb ran head-on into a North Alabama buzzsaw. That buzzsaw was named Israel Pickens, the leader of the North Carolina faction, and he wanted a state bank.

Bibb and his followers favored the private banks. The issue divided them like a cleaver, along with the north-south, Georgia-North Carolina loyalties.

The North Carolina-North Alabama faction took

charge in 1821, when Pickens was elected governor, after he took the cause of the have-nots against the privileged few.

Now the state was set for political rivalry that has continued through the years, down to this very day.

In North Alabama were the plain people, looking to Gen. Andrew Jackson for leadership. In South Alabama were the planters, the aristocrats, who thought they were born to lead.

They fought over the location of the capital. The Georgians won with St. Stephens as territorial capital, the North Carolinians won with Huntsville as temporary capital, and the Georgians snatched control back with the selection of Cahaba as permanent capital.

When Cahaba failed as a capital because of the flood prone Cahaba River—when it flooded, they rowed to the state capitol in rowboats—the North Alabama faction grabbed control again, moving the capital to Tuscaloosa.

And finally, South Alabama grabbed the capital shortly before the Civil War and moved it to Montgomery—in South Alabama, on the Alabama River.

The factions fought over secession in 1860, with the South Alabamians (who had more slaves) fighting for Alabama to walk out of the Union, and the North Alabama faction fighting to stay in the Union.

It was a close fight in the Secession Convention of 1861. But, by a margin of 61-39 (a preliminary vote was much closer: 53-45), the delegates voted to secede.

They fought over representation—South Alabama refusing to reapportion the Legislature as the population shifted north, and North Alabama demanding more representation.

The battle over representation went on until the U.S. Supreme Court resolved it with the "one-man, one-vote" decision of the 1960s.

So the pattern of Alabama politics was set for 160 years by the forces boiling on the frontier of 1820. And a stumbling horse may have quickened the change.

Marquis de LaFayette

Chapter Five

1825

Hail the Hero! LaFayette visits Alabama

It was a strange sight.

From the Georgia bank of the Chattahoochee, about a dozen miles down river from present-day Phenix City, the wooden ferry crunched into the mud.

An old man, dressed in the uniform of an American major general, stepped into the boat.

Immediately he was surrounded by 50 leaping Indian warriors, described as "stripped naked and finely painted." The Indians jostled each other in a frenzy, each trying to touch the old man.

Then, after all the warriors had touched him, they fell silent and retired to the bow of the ferry. As the boat touched the Alabama bank of the river, the leader of the Indians cut loose with a piercing whoop. The warriors repeated it, with gusto.

Then the Indians seized the old man and put him in a sulky, a cross between a carriage and a gun caisson. Sixty Indians then hitched themselves to the sulky and pulled it—in absolute silence—to the top of a knoll overlooking the river.

Here, all the Indians came forward and rubbed their forearms against the forearm of the old man. It was the traditional greeting of the Creeks.

Then the leader of the Indians turned the old man over to a delegation of white men, waiting on the top of the knoll.

It was a day in early April of 1825, and Alabama was welcoming a hero of the American Revolution. His name: Marie Joseph Paul Ives Roch Gilbert du Motier, Marquis de LaFayette.

Born to French nobility, the young marquis was orphaned at 13, when he inherited a huge fortune. He married at 16, and his wife brought another fortune with her. He entered the Guards, and was a captain of dragoons at 19.

Then, in 1776 he heard that the English colonies in America had proclaimed their independence. "At the first news of this quarrel," he wrote afterwards, "my heart was enrolled in it."

Not only his heart, but his fortune, his reputation, his very life. Disobeying orders from the French king, he outfitted a ship, loaded it with supplies and volunteers, and headed for America.

In America, General Washington liked the dashing young French officer, and formed a lifelong friendship with him. Washington gave him a place on his staff, and LaFayette was in the war.

He believed in America with all his heart, and his touching faith in the American cause brought him even closer to Washington.

Before long, Washington pinned a general's stars on Lafayette's shoulders, and gave him command of an American division. He was wounded in the first battle of Brandywine.

When he recovered, he fought on with Washington through the rest of the war, and was on hand at Yorktown, when the British stacked their rifles and came out to surrender to the tune of "The World Turned Upside Down."

LaFayette had a great deal to do with bringing France into the war on the side of America, and probably helped place the French fleet off the mouth of Chesapeake Bay, which put the cork in the bottle and trapped Cornwallis at Yorktown.

After the Revolutionary War, LaFayette went home to France, and played a major role in the French Revolution. He served for a time as commander of the National Guard of France.

He steadfastly stood for liberty through the turbulent years after the French Revolution, and was jailed in Prussia and Austria.

Napoleon Bonaparte won a battle in 1797, and wrote LaFayette's release into the treaty signed after the battle.

As a member of the French chamber of deputies, he voted against the life consulate of Napoleon, and against the imperial title for him. From 1818 to 1824 he was a deputy, always voting against the imperial Napoleon.

Then in July of 1824, LaFayette came back to America for a triumphal tour. From July of 1824 until September of 1825, he ranged over America, always to the cheers of the people.

A grateful America gave him $200,000 and a huge tract of land, a whole township. His visit seemed to set

off an outpouring of love from the Americans—here
was a man who had loved them and risked his life for
them, when he and their country were both young.

Down the eastern seaboard he came, with balls
and parties and celebrations every time his carriage
creaked to a stop. Through Georgia, across the
Chattahoochee, to Alabama. He had been traveling for
10 months, bumping along on bad roads.

The leader of the Creeks held out his hand toward
the knot of waiting men on the knoll.

"General LaFayette, the American friend," said
the Indian, pointing to the old man. Then he pointed to
the leader of the Alabama delegation. "Mr. Hall of
Alabama."

He was greeted by Bolling Hall, a former congressman and a Revolutionary War soldier.

There were speeches, the Indians played a frantic
ball game, whacking each other with their sticks, and
LaFayette headed for Montgomery.

The capital of Alabama was Cahaba, located down
river from Montgomery, and a delegation—led by Gov.
Israel Pickens—had come to Montgomery to greet the
old warrior.

Governor Pickens, a timid man, was intimidated
by the presence of the great man and could not get a
word out. But Bolling Hall, who made the speech at
Fort Mitchell on the Chattahoochee, took up the slack
and made the welcoming speech.

Governor Pickens' shyness made have been inten-
sified because one of the members of the escort, an
Indian trader named Thomas Carr, fell in a well and
had to be rescued before LaFayette could be properly
welcomed.

More festivities, another ball, and the LaFayette
party got on a boat for Cahaba, the capital. More balls,
more festivities, more cheers. Then on to Claiborne,
down river on the Alabama, and finally to Mobile.

At Mobile, more cheers, more festivities, more

speeches, another great ball. During the ball, an onlooker rushed into the room and—either in a spirit of mischief or possibly under the influence of strong drink—yelled "FIRE!"

The spectators ran for the nearest exits. General LaFayette, seeing no exit nearby, jumped out a window and landed in a mud puddle.

It is said that his major general's uniform "was the worse for wear from being mud-spattered when he landed in Royal Street."

After a few more hours of partying, the seemingly inexhaustible LaFayette boarded a ship for New Orleans. He would travel for another five or six months before returning to France.

He died in Paris on May 20, 1834. The Americans sent earth from Bunker Hill to cover his grave.

William Barret Travis

Chapter Six

1831

Hero of the Alamo
On run from Alabama

The long line of horsemen, broken by the creaking of an occasional buggy, moved through the scrub pine of Monroe County, that day in 1831.

One of the horsemen wiped his face with a handkerchief. He was William Barret Travis, a 22-year-old lawyer who lived in Claiborne, then the county seat of Monroe County.

The others were members of "the circuit," a traveling group of lawyers, clerks and a judge, moving from frontier town to frontier town, trying cases and dispensing rough-hewn justice.

The pines thinned out, and the outlines of a cluster of log houses and a dirt street opened up through the woods. Travis spurred his horse forward, to arrive early at the inn.

Members of the traveling court had dinner at the inn, amidst legal jokes and bluffs about who would do what to whom in the courtroom the next day, and they all went to their rooms for the night

The moon swung up and over the pines, and a dim figure moved alongside the log walls of the inn, keeping to the shadows.

Travis had crept from his room, and he moved toward the corral where the horses muttered to themselves. He saddled his horse silently, eased out of the town, and galloped the sweating horse back home to Claiborne.

Sure enough, just as he suspected, he found his wife with another man. He killed the man and swore his wife to silence. Then he galloped back through the shadowy pines, unsaddled his blowing horse, and crept back into the bed at the inn.

Next morning, he joined the others for breakfast, and they joked with him about looking sleepy. Yawning, he conferred with his clients before taking them before the judge.

Back in Claiborne, another man—an unsavory character known to be a gambler—was arrested for the killing and charged with murder. Weeks later, the case came to court.

Travis, the real killer, watched from the audience as the trial went on. There was strong evidence; it appeared that the gambler would be convicted.

When court adjourned, Travis went home and packed a few belongings and ordered a mulatto man-servant, Ben Travis, to saddle two horses.

He then went to the home of the judge and made him promise—on his oath as a fellow Mason—that he would not act on the information he would give the judge—at least not for a few hours.

The judge gave him his word. He would not act immediately on the information. Then Travis told him: He had killed the man, because he had caught him with his wife. The judge sat there, stunned, unable to act.

Travis got up from his chair, walked outside, got on his horse, and disappeared, along with his manservant Ben.

Travis was born in Red Banks, S. C., in 1809. He came to Alabama as a youth with his parents, Mark Travis and Jemima Stallworth Travis. He studied law with a Judge Dellet and was admitted to the bar at Claiborne. He married Rosanna E. Cato and they had two children, a son an a daughter.

On the day he disappeared, Travis crossed the Alabama River and headed for a new country. Texas. Alabama law—or U.S. law—could not touch him there.

In Texas, Travis gained prominence as a lawyer, a politician and a soldier.

On Feb. 23, 1836, Lt. Col. William Barret Travis commanded a small group of of 155 soldiers at the Alamo, a former mission, then a fort, in San Antonio.

There was dust on the horizon, and soon the horsemen of the Mexican army appeared, surrounding The Alamo (the name pertains to the cottonwoods which grew nearby).

"Surrender!" demanded Santa Anna, the Mexican commander, "or I will give no quarter."

"I shall never surrender or retreat," barked Travis, and the siege was on.

Travis sent for help—shadowy figures sneaking from the fort, running to tell Gen. Sam Houston of his plight.

A relief column, only a few men, drove through the encircling Mexicans, but they were of little help. Travis now had 188 men inside, with 3,000 to 5,000 Mexicans outside.

The Mexican artillery hammered the fort mercilessly. The Texans stopped firing from the walls, bent
on conserving ammunition, waiting for the Mexican
assault to come.

The Mexicans, yelling as they came, stormed the
walls. They were driven back. Another attack, and they
were beaten back again.

Then, shortly before 5 a.m., they came again.
There were bugles, and the rockets, and the yelling as
they came closer.

Travis waited at the north battery, directing his
artillery and holding a shotgun.

"Come on, boys, the Mexicans are upon us and
we'll give them hell," shouted Travis, peering into the
darkness.

The Mexicans stormed across a protective ditch,
now too close for the artillery to bear on them, and some
of the soldiers leaned planks—for climbing—against
the wall of the Alamo.

Travis leaned over the parapet and boomed his
shotgun into the faces of the climbing Mexicans. There
was a volley of fire from the darkness, and a pistol ball
caught Travis in the head. He fell back, mortally
wounded.

The Mexicans stormed over the wall, killing everyone as they came. The Texans, without a commander and almost without ammunition, fought back
using their rifles as clubs.

When the slaughter was over, the dead Texans
littered the courtyard. There was Davy Crockett, the
loud-mouthed Tennessee Indian fighter who had told
his last tall tale, and Col. James Bowie, he of the deadly
broad-bladed knife, and co-commander with Travis at
the Alamo before he got sick.

And there was William Barret Travis, a crumpled
dead figure on the wall—born a South Carolinian, who
grew up as an Alabamian, now forever a Texan.

When they heard of his death at the Alamo, two of

his brothers—Jim and Mark—left Alabama for Texas to avenge their brother. Jim's horse fell, breaking Jim's leg, and Mark took him back home, then set out for Texas alone.

Only a few weeks after the Alamo, Santa Anna and his Mexican army were chasing Sam Houston and his Texas army. At a place called San Jacinto, during the Mexican midday siesta, Houston turned and savagely attacked the Mexicans.

Santa Anna was beaten, his army scattered and Texas was free. As the Texans swung into battle that day, they shouted: "Remember the Alamo!"

Brother Mark Travis returned from Texas with a head wound and was regarded as "rather queer" in Alabama after that.

Family historians say he was clerk of the court, and, not caring to bother with written court, merely "carried everything in his head." People regarded him as brilliant, as he spouted court records on command.

Mark died, the Civil War came and went, and during the occupation of the South after the war, his widow disgraced the family by marrying the Yankee colonel attached to a nearby Federal garrison.

"The people," says one family historian, "quit speaking to her."

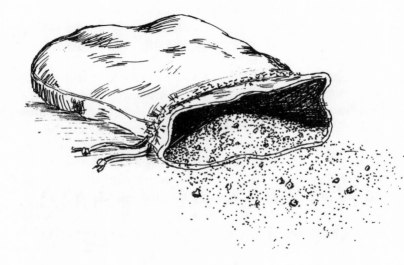

Chapter Seven

1832

————

GOLD IN ALABAMA!
Blared the newspaper,
And gold rush was on

A million years ago, the crust of the earth twisted as if in pain.

There was a shudder and a scraping moan deep in the earth, and a jagged slab of granite and quartz, 50 miles long, was born. It pushed itself up above the land that was to become Alabama.

The Devil's Backbone, they called it later. It stretched from Elmore County to the northeast, through Tallapoosa and into Chambers County.

Hundreds of thousands of years went by. Giant ferns unfolded like trees, and withered. Dinosaurs flourished and died in the bogs. There were drowning sheets of rain, and killing heat, and great snows that piled up against the jagged outcropping of rock.

But the 50-mile slab endured.

Nature attacked it. The rains washed away some of the loose rock. Slivers of water trickled deep into the cracks. When the water expanded into ice, the rocks cracked open.

The searching fingers of plant roots probed into the faults of the rock, looking for a weak spot. The roots grew, and the rock split.

As the crystalline quartz rocks broke open, tiny particles of shiny metal spilled out onto the ground.

One day in 1830, a white man pulled his canoe up on a sandbar in the Tallapoosa River, and he noticed the bright flecks in the sand.

About the same time, a bearded trader led his mule up the side of the Devil's Backbone, and he saw the same bright flecks shining out of the face of the rock.

On May 16, 1832, several newspapers in North-eastern cities trumpeted the news: GOLD IN ALA-BAMA!

The rush began. City slickers from Philadelphia appeared on mules, with top hats strapped on behind. Farmers from North Carolina and Virginia, tired of the plow and the hoe, appeared with that wild gold look in their eyes. Gamblers, prostitutes, preachers, doctors, storekeepers, blacksmiths, they all came.

Gold towns sprang up, with muddy streets and clapboard shacks. There was Arbacoochee and Chulafinnee in Cleburne, Pinatucky and Pinkneyville in Randolph, Ida in Clay, Riddle's Mill in Talladega, and Devil's Backbone and Goldville in Tallapoosa County.

In Arbacoochee, there were 20 general stores, five

saloons, two hotels, a fire department, 100 permanent homes and a race track. There were 600 people working in the gold fields near Arbacoochee, and it was one of the largest towns in Alabama.

Men worked the streams with gold pans; they built sluices and cradles, and burrowed into the rock, looking for gold. And they found it. There were nuggets, worth about $1,200 each, and a steady stream of gold dust strained from the earth.

The storekeepers kept their gold dust in hollow turkey quills, carefully tucked away in a secret place.

A German named Ullrich had bought some land near Goldville from the Indians and he wanted to start a vineyard. He planted some grapes, then gold was discovered on his land. He forgot his grapes and began digging for the golden dream.

His neighbors misunderstood his heavy German accent and thought he was Dutch. So they called his place the Dutch Bend Mine.

Sharpsters came, with their marked cards and their loaded dice. And there were brawls in the muddy streets. Undertakers did a flourishing business.

A con man would take the pellets out of a shotgun shell, and load it with particles of gold. The shotgun blast embedded the pieces of gold into a rocky hillside, and then the con man carefully allowed the gold to be "discovered."

Then he stood back as the miners lined up to buy parcels of his land. Shortly thereafter, he left town, before the miners discovered they had bought a pile of worthless rocks.

Other con men would "salt" the ground, as they called it, sprinkle bits of the glittery metal over a piece of ground and wait for it to be "discovered."

Through the late 1830s, and deep into the 1840s, Alabama's gold towns prospered. Over in Georgia, at Dahlonega, the U.S. government set up a mint to coin the flow of gold.

In the Alabama gold fields, there was never an all-out showering of wealth coming down on the gold-seekers. There was a trickle, sometimes a steady flow, of gold coming out of the Alabama hills. But the gold rush fever, the wild-eyed hope of finding enormous wealth just around the bend in the road, diminished and faded. The extracting of gold from the earth became a job, a living.

Then, one day in 1849, came the death knell for Alabama's gold towns.

GOLD IN CALIFORNIA! the headline blared. The news of Sutter's Mill spread through the Alabama gold fields like brushfire, and gold-hungry miners of Arbacoochee and Chulafinnee, of Devil's Backbone and Goldville, packed up their shovels and pans, and headed for the promised land on the shores of the Pacific Ocean.

A few short years after, most of the Alabama gold towns were abandoned, shells of empty houses and saloons with spider webs behind the bars.

And behind the creaking doors and the crumbling walls, the ghosts of empty dreams. The Alabama Gold Rush was over.

In the Alabama gold fields, there was never an all-out showering of wealth coming down on the goldseekers. There was a trickle, sometimes a steady flow, of gold coming out of the Alabama hills. But the gold rush fever, the wild-eyed hope of finding enormous wealth just around the bend in the road, diminished and faded.

Sam Houston

Chapter Eight

1832

An Alabama belle Tamed San Houston, Hero of San Jacinto

The brass band struck up a brave tune, and the crowd on the New Orleans dock craned their necks to see their hero.

The boat came alongside the dock, and they lifted him to bring him ashore. Matted hair, bloodshot eyes, tangled beard, strips of bloody shirt wrapped around a shattered ankle.

The band stopped playing, the brave tune died on the summer air, and mouths dropped open in surprise.

This was Sam Houston? This was the victor over the Mexicans in the Battle of San Jacinto, authentic American hero?

As the general was lifted onto a litter, his eyes rolled and he fainted. In the crowd, a 17-year-old schoolgirl from Marion, Ala., cried at the sight. It was May 22, 1836. The schoolgirl was Margaret Lea.

Houston, recuperating in New Orleans from battle wounds, already had lived a full life in his 43 years. Born in Virginia, he grew up on the Tennessee frontier. He ran away from home at 15, and spent three years among the Cherokees.

He enlisted to serve with Gen. Andrew Jackson, and fought at the Battle of Horseshoe Bend on the Tallapoosa River in 1814. Later, he became governor of Tennessee, then his wife left him and he resigned as governor.

Moving to Texas, he organized an army against the Mexicans and became its commander. He captured Santa Anna, the Mexican commander who had slaughtered Americans at the Alamo, and Mexico recognized the independence of Texas.

But Houston was wounded in his hour of glory, and he came to New Orleans to recuperate.

Houston went on to become president of Texas, finally getting Texas in the Union in 1845.

But it was in May of 1839, three years after they carried him off the boat in New Orleans, that Houston first saw Margaret Lea.

She was visiting relatives in Mobile, and Houston came to visit her sister's house.

Houston mistook her for her sister, and said to a friend: "If she were not already married, I'd give that charming lady a chance to say no."

That's the unmarried sister you were talking to, the friend told him. "So you are free to give her the chance, General."

Houston stayed with her sister's family for a week,

making talks about land values in Texas, trying to lure investors to his state. Each evening, Margaret sat at the piano, playing and singing songs to him. The General was smitten.

One evening, according to one biographer, Houston pointed to a lone star low in the heavens. It was his star of destiny, he told Margaret, and he asked her to look at it after he was gone.

She was to remember, he told her, about life in Texas. It was the most beautiful country in the world, but not without hardship. He was going to Nashville to see his old friend Andrew Jackson, and he would write to her.

Margaret's family frowned on the romance. Houston was too old. He was 47, she was 21. She was a devout Baptist, cultured, educated and with a flair for writing. He was a rough pioneer, had little use for churches, shouted profane language like a fountain, and absorbed whiskey like a sponge.

As promised, Houston wrote to her from Tennessee, and watched the postman like a lovesick schoolboy for her reply. Soon it came, a letter from an innocent, sheltered girl in love for the first time in her life.

He came back through Alabama on his way to Texas, and visited Margaret at her home in Marion. When he left for Texas, he was smiling. She had promised to be his wife.

Later, someone asked her why she had risked all in the face of the warnings she had been given about Houston. "He won my heart," she said.

In Texas, Houston pleaded with her by mail: Come to Texas. She wrote back, giving the date when she would arrive. But when the boat docked in Galveston, Houston charged aboard, only to find Margaret's stern-faced mother.

"General Houston," said the frowning woman, "My daughter is in Alabama. She goes forth in the world to marry no man. The man who receives her hand will receive it in my home, and not elsewhere."

A month later, Mrs. Lea went back to Alabama. Houston meekly followed. At Marion, he rode horseback out to the Lea home, reined in his horse, and asked for Margaret's hand in the parlor.

Then came a shock. The family insisted he tell them about his first wife, Eliza Allen, who had left him.

Houston, tight-lipped, strode from the Lea house and rode back into Marion.

But soon he was back again, and told them how Miss Allen had married him at her parents' insistence, even though she told them she loved someone else. That satisfied the family.

On May 9, 1840, Margaret Moffette Lea and Sam Houston were married at the home of her brother, Henry Lea, on Greensboro Road in Marion. At a public dinner for the distinguished visitor, the presiding officer offered a toast: "I give you ... the Conqueress of the Conquerer ... Mrs. Margaret M. Houston."

From Marion, the Houstons went to Mobile, New Orleans and Galveston. On the way, Margaret told her new husband her view on temperance. The general agreed. He would never drink to excess again.

In 1841, Houston again became president of Texas, and for the next 25 years, Margaret Houston's life was tied up in the political affairs of Texas.

They had eight children, four boys and four girls, and Margaret Houston devoted her life to her family.

Houston worked to get Texas into his beloved Union. After admission in 1845, he served as U.S. senator from Texas from 1846 to 1859.

With war clouds boiling on the horizon, Houston disagreed with other Southerners in Congress. They yelled for secession, he wanted Texas to stay in the Union, not leave it.

In 1859, he ran for governor of Texas on a "stay in the Union" platform and won the election. But in 1861, Texas voted to pull out of the Union, and it broke

Houston's heart.

Houston refused to lead his state out of the Union, and Confederates removed him from office.

Although strongly opposed to secession, Houston sadly gave his permission for his eldest son to join the Confederate army. The son died two years later, in the midst of the war his father had tried to stop.

Mrs. Houston, after her husband's death, moved to Independence, Tex., where her mother then lived.

In 1867, a yellow fever epidemic broke out, and Mrs. Houston worked day and night at the bedsides of the stricken people of her town.

At the age of 48, Margaret Lea Houston, one of Alabama's greatest daughters, died in Texas, a victim of yellow fever.

Francis Scott Key

Chapter Nine

1833

Star Spangled Banner Author kept Alabama Out of rebellion

Twenty eight years before the guns boomed at Fort Sumter to begin the Civil War, Alabama stood on the brink of an "almost civil war" with the federal government.

And it took a visit by Francis Scott Key, composer of *The Star Spangled Banner*, to calm the troubled waters.

It was a hot day—that last day of July of 1833— when the breathless Indians came running to the federal marshal on the Chattahoochee River: The white man had stolen their fields, he had killed their hogs and horses, and he had beaten some of the Indians badly.

The marshal, Jeremiah Austill (who had fought with Sam Dale in the bloody "Canoe Fight" of 1813, chronicled in Volume I of Mr. Stallworth's Alabama history series, *A Day In The Life of Alabama*), rode over to see the white man, Hardeman Owens of Russell County.

After listening to Owens, Austill ordered him to leave the Creek Nation—a huge bloc of territory in East Alabama—and Owens' temper boiled over. He would die first, he told Austill.

Austill, his authority questioned and his face red, went off to Fort Mitchell and came back with a detachment of soldiers.

Owens eyed the U.S. soldiers with hatred, and promised with clenched teeth that he would leave. Austill turned his soldiers around and headed back for the fort, about a dozen miles down river from present-day Phenix City on the Chattahoochee.

But on the way back, they were overtaken by excited Indians. Owens had threatened to burn their homes and kill anyone who dared to come onto the fields he had taken from them.

When the angry Austill returned, Owens had sent his family away and had set a mine—a pile of gunpowder in his house. As the marshal rode up to the gate of the house, an Indian whispered to Austill that Owens had set a trap.

Just at that moment, Owens broke and ran from the back of the house, and the house exploded, fragments of wood flying through the air.

Finally, a detachment of soldiers cornered Owens and ordered him to surrender. Owens angrily shook his head, and pulled a pistol. He aimed it at the sergeant in command, and one of the soldiers cut him down with a single rifle shot.

The flame of anger swept through the neighboring counties, then through the entire state. Mass meetings were held, resolutions were passed, and plans were made to raise a militia force to fight the federal soldiers.

In Lowndes County a resolution passed amidst the shouts of a mass meeting. It said that "the removal of our citizens from their settlements by force is unconstitutional, oppressive and utterly subversive of the sovereignty of the state, and we cannot and will not submit to it."

Federal troops massed at Fort Mitchell, gearing up to meet the threat of armed rebellion, and Alabama was poised on the brink of war.

It was a peculiar situation—a huge chunk of territory, the Creek Nation, governed by federal treaty and federal authority, inside a state, governed by state laws.

It was an indigestible federal lump in the stomach of an angry state, a governmental upset stomach.

The situation began years before, when Gen. Andrew Jackson broke the power of the Creeks at Horseshoe Bend, in 1814. By the terms of the Treaty of Fort Jackson, the Indians were confined to their fields and forests east of the Coosa River and north of a line going southwest from Wetumpka to a point below Eufaula (then called Irwinton).

Under the Treaty of Cusseta in 1832, the Creek Nation existed inside the state of Alabama—the counties of Russell, Macon, Lee, Clay, Tallapoosa, Cleburne, Calhoun, and parts of Barbour, Bullock and Elmore.

But the Treaty of Cusseta, ratified in 1832, provided that the Creeks "cede to the United States all their lands east of the Mississippi River." It also provided that all white settlers would be removed from the Creek Nation.

It was this thorny provision which caused the trouble, because white settlers had drifted into the Creek Nation territory, and pretty much taken over the lands they wanted—and let the Indians holler.

They did take the land, illegally, and the Indians did holler.

Gov. John Gayle of Alabama pushed for, and signed, an act of the general assembly which carved nine new counties out of the Creek Nation—Coosa, Benton (now Calhoun), Talladega, Tallapoosa, Russell, Randolph, Chambers, Macon and Barbour.

State laws now applied—as of December of 1832— over these counties, said Gayle.

The governor, in a letter to the federal government, said the Indians in these counties had become citizens of Alabama. He said the federal government could make no treaty which went against the right of the state to jurisdiction inside its territorial boundaries.

Was the Creek Nation to be governed by the U.S. government? Or come under the laws of the State of Alabama?

The thing came to a head with the killing of Hardeman Owens, and war seemed bound to happen.

But then Gayle wrote a letter to the settlers (there were about 25,000 settlers in the disputed lands by now) and asked them for restraint, and to settle their differences by laws instead of guns.

The dash of cold water worked. Tempers subsided, and the troops stayed in Fort Mitchell.

So President Jackson in Washington, perplexed by the problem, asked a U.S. Attorney to go to Alabama and iron things out. He was Francis Scott Key, the author of the national anthem.

Key came to Tuscaloosa, then the capital of the state, and felt the heat of the situation. He then sent Governor Gayle his offer:

The federal government would complete the surveys in the Indian territory by Jan. 15, 1834, and the government would make no removals of white settlers outside these allotments in the survey.

Also, Key said, the settlers would have the power

to buy the Indian lands they occupied.

Key's proposal meant the U.S. government had backed down. It would withdraw the federal order for the removal of the white settlers. And it was a victory for the state—Alabama had the right to exercise sovereignty over territory within its boundaries.

The Key proposals were never adopted by the Alabama General Assembly, but they assumed the force of fact through public opinion and the re-election of Governor Gayle, who had backed them.

The 'final solution" of the Creek problem waited on the back burner until the so-called Creek War in 1836, when the Creek Nation was erased, and the Creeks sent on the tearful road to exile, the "Trail of Tears" to the alien lands of Oklahoma

The tact and skill of Francis Scott Key, however, may have averted a bloody prelude to full-scale civil war—28 years before the guns of Sumter boomed.

Chapter Ten

1834

Students shoot
At University president

The University of Alabama students, dressed in white, were out on the prowl.

Waving their pistols, they roamed the campus that night, looking for Rev. Alva Woods, president of the University.

Then they found him—a bald, thirtyish man—coming into a dormitory.

They began to throw brickbats at him. He ran and, as he turned the corner of the house, a pistol was fired in his direction. He found an open window and jumped in it.

This happened one night in 1834, three years after the University opened on April 12, 1831.

But the first official step toward the creation of the University happened before Alabama became a state in 1819.

It was on April 20, 1818, when the U.S. Congress passed a law which said "there shall be reserved in the sale of lands in the Alabama territory a township for the support of a seminary of learning within the said territory."

That "seminary of learning" was to become the University of Alabama.

When Alabama became a state in 1819, Gov. William Wyatt Bibb was authorized to appoint commissioners to sell the land and look for a site for the University.

In 1822, the board of trustees narrowed the choices—Athens, Autauga County, Wilson Hill in Shelby County, Gages in Perry County, and Tuscaloosa.

But the Legislature didn't act until December of 1827, when it selected Tuscaloosa as the place for the "seminary of learning."

The state capital had just been moved from Cahaba to Tuscaloosa and the legislators, meeting in Tuscaloosa, may have been influenced by this.

The trustees began selling the land given them by Congress, at a going rate of $17 an acre. Sales were held in Cahaba, at the Big Spring in Franklin County, and at Tuscaloosa.

Now, with a site chosen, where in Tuscaloosa County would they put the school? The candidates were Marr's Field, the Childers Place, and the Taber place.

The trustees chose Marr's Field for several reasons: There was clay there, to make brick; plenty of timber there, and good sandstone available for columns and foundations (the quarry can still be seen on the north side of the campus). And there was water—

Marr's Spring served as the university's water supply for almost 100 years.

It doesn't appear in the minutes, but it was clear that Marr's Field—a mile and a half from the town—was far enough away to keep the "unruly" students from going to town a lot.

The state architect, Capt. William Nichols, was chosen to design the buildings. The original estimate for building the university was $56,000, and it took about three years to build.

Much of the construction was done by slaves, but some stone masons were from Scotland.

Where the Gorgas Library now stands was the site of the most impressive of the buildings—the Rotunda. It was round, three stories high, topped by a golden dome and surrounded by 24 pillars. Inside were lecture rooms, the library, the auditorium and a museum.

Behind the Rotunda, standing where Clark Hall is today, stood the Lyceum, two stories high with a portico of six Ionic columns. It housed classrooms and the chemistry lab.

Opening day was April 12, 1831, when the crowd gathered in the Episcopal Church in Tuscaloosa.

Gov. Samuel B. Moore gave what was called a "neat, brief, sensible and to the purpose" speech and handed the keys to the university to a bald-headed Yankee who looked down his nose at some of the frontier ways of his students—the Rev. Alva Woods, first president of the university.

Taking the keys, the stern Woods spelled out his plans. He was a Baptist preacher, had been student at Harvard and had been president of Transylvania College.

A Tuscaloosa newspaper, *The Spirit of the Age*, gave this account.:

"President Woods then delivered his inaugural address. The leading subject of the discourse was the importance of learning and knowledge to the safety, liberty, prosperity and moral and religious improvement of man.

"In the progress of the discourse, the speaker addressed the board of trustees in particular, and among other things reminded them of the importance of husbanding the resources of the institution and regarding them as sacred to the cause of learning and the diffusion of knowledge."

President Woods made no secret of it. He was going to be a tough disciplinarian, and if the students didn't like it, they could go home.

But the students, who began to trickle into the town April 18, came mostly from the free and easy plantation life in Alabama.

Many of them were more interested in gambling and drinking than they were in school books.

Fresh from the buckskin of frontier life, the students were poorly prepared for serious academic studies. Not only that, they disliked Yankee professors.

The stern-faced Woods was unyielding. He told the students they were lawless characters, and denounced their parents for sending him such roughnecks.

The students listened, sneered at the prissy Yankee president, and went on their roughneck ways. At one point, students barricaded the door of an unpopular Yankee professor and put a blower on top his chimney, to smoke him out.

Red-eyed from the smoke, he found he could not open his door. Then he raised a window to get some air, and the students threw rocks at him.

There were only about 100 students that first year, but Woods and teachers averaged expelling more than a student a week.

The rough house continued. Students threw a rooster into the classroom of mild-mannered Professor Saltonstall. When the rooster attacked the professor, he calmly wrung the chicken's neck.

After whiskey was discovered in his room, a student named George Lister assaulted a professor with a deadly weapon. Another student, Thomas Jefferson Gordon, was expelled for attacking a professor.

Students also were expelled for such offenses as attending a circus. By the 1840s, students had been charged with everything from the destruction of a Bible in the Rotunda to the discharge of firearms and the use of blasphemous language on the college grounds.

They were also charged with surrounding a seminary for young ladies, and insulting and alarming the inmates with boisterous shouts, profane language and the discharge of firearms.

But the clearest picture of the rowdy students comes from one of the students. Clement Clay, writing to his father in 1834, said:

"Matters have been growing worse every day, 'til on Saturday night there was an open and audacious rebellion. About 10 students collected at the sound of a horn, and commenced dressing themselves in white.

"Mr. Hutchins (a teacher) ran into the room in which they were, and, succeeding in detecting two or three, left them and returned to his room. A bottle was thrown after him but it did not strike him.

"Soon after this dispersion they met again with their horns and tin pans, and with pistols and clubs, commenced firing, shouting, etc. Mr. Tutwiler (another teacher) went out to them, and they left him and came in pursuit of Dr. Woods.

"They met him coming into the dormitory and began to throw brickbats at him. He ran, and as he turned the corner of the house, a pistol was fired in the direction towards him. He availed himself of an open window and jumped in it.

"They, fortunately, on turning the corner, ran around to the opposite side of the house, and, not seeing him, went into the cellars and then out into the woods to find him. He then came out and went to his own room without a light.

"The insurgents by this time had added 10 to their number and returned. Unable to find him, they rocked his window and finally started upstairs to take him out if he should be there. But Woods was in another room, and they then went down and paraded on the campus.

"Dr. Wallis (another teacher) came out, and they told him if he approached it was at his own peril, cocking their pistols at the same time. They broke in the chapel and rung the bell, stoned Mr. Wallis' window, and about 1 a.m. stillness was procured by their own drowsiness."

Some teachers were held up as scapegoats and fired. By 1836, most of the original teachers had been forced to leave.

In 1837, there was another change, which brought cheers from the students.

Rev. Alva Woods packed his books and left, shaking his head over what he must have thought were common rowdies.

He had tried to form a great institution of learning, but his strict methods and the free and easy ways of the frontier lit a powder keg of controversy.

After this stormy start, the University of Alabama went on to gather a reputation as a great institution of learning.

But underneath—with the reverberations of the rowdies chasing the president through a dormitory window—it never quite gave up its reputation as a party school.

Rev. Alva Woods packed his books and left, shaking his head over what he must have thought were common rowdies.

Menawa

Chapter Eleven

1835

Menawa touches land One last time, then Walks Trail of Tears

His Creek braves called him Great Warrior.

In his youth, because of his slashing recklessness against the white men on the Tennessee frontier, he had been called Hothlepoya, Crazy War Hunter.

But wisdom had come with age, and now this square-faced, bulb-nosed man stood inside the log barricade at Cholocco Itabixee, the Horse's Flat Foot, a loop in the Tallapoosa River.

His name: Menawa.

With the barricade, the Indians now called the river bend Tohopeka, The Fort. It was either an impregnable fortress or a death trap. The Americans called it Horseshoe Bend.

Beyond the logs, across the long sward of a clearing, Menawa could see the American soldiers gathering, and the man on the horse who led them—the Indians called him Old Mad Jackson—Gen. Andrew Jackson of Tennessee.

Inside the barricade, Menawa—second in command—was having troubles. The first chief and prophet—Monahell—had awakened, dressed in all his finery, and had gone into a hypnotic trance, trying to put his "medicine" on the white troops.

Then came the word: Jackson's troops had broken into the loop of the river, in the rear of the Creek warriors, and now they were moving in closer behind them.

Monahell ordered his troops to abandon the log barricade and attack to their rear. Menawa, the Great Warrior, shook his head. He knew better than to trust the prophet's "medicine" against the lead balls and steel bayonets of the Americans. The barricade was their only chance, and they must hold it.

Menawa ran to the prophet, and killed him with one blow. Then he ordered the warriors to hold the barricade against the hard-charging Americans.

It was just thirty minutes past noon on March 27, 1814, when the American troops reached the barricade.

Menawa jumped into the fray, shouting the Creek war whoop. He fought hard, with rifle first, then with bloody tomahawk and war club.

The battle raged up and down the logs. There was bloody hand-to-hand combat, until about 3:30 p.m. Menawa was shot seven times, once through the head, and continued to fight until he collapsed. He was covered with the bodies of Creek warriors, but he was determined never to give up.

Now the battle was over, and the American swept the field with their bayonets. The Indians knew they were fighting for their national life. None surrendered, and they were killed systematically, mercilessly.

At nightfall, the sporadic fighting stopped, and Jackson stood victor on the battlefield. The Battle of Horseshoe Bend broke the back of the Creeks. It smashed their power, and it catapulted Jackson into national prominence. And the road to the White House opened up before him.

For Menawa, it was the beginning the end. He pulled himself from the tangle of Creek bodies, crawled to the bank of the river. He hid himself in a canoe, and drifted down river to safety.

Menawa lived from the time the Creeks held sway over much of Georgia and Alabama, until the time when they were kicked out and pushed across the Mississippi to new lands.

The whole tragedy of the Indians in the Southeast is contained in his life.

When he was born, in the late 1800s, the Creek Nation was a power—50 towns stretching along the Coosa and Tallapossa, and along the Flint (in western Georgia) and the Chattahoochee (dividing line between Alabama Georgia today). The towns were joined by a yearly meeting, governing the overall nation.

As a child, Menawa watched Alexander McGillivray (the Indians called him Hoboi-Hili-Micco, the Good Child King) gather the power of the Creeks, uniting their towns into a nation, or confederacy. And he used the concentrated power to slow the western march of the whites.

McGillivray, a half-blood son of an Indian princess and a Scottish trader, parlayed with the Spanish, the English, and the Americans, to keep all of them off balance. He welded the Creeks into a single unit and held the threat of Indian war over the heads of the settlers.

In 1790, McGillivray went to New York, then the capital of the United States. He signed a treaty with President George Washington, all the while continuing secret negotiations with the Spanish in Pensacola. The Spanish held Florida and West Florida, which included Mobile and the lower part of present-day Alabama.

The Good Child King died in 1793 of a mysterious disease and his death left a power vacuum which was impossible to fill. The Creek nation began to break up.

Then, in 1811, the great Shawnee chief Tecumseh, backed by the English, came south from Ohio, urging an all-out war against the encroaching whites.

Menawa stood among the chiefs, and there were 5,000 braves gathered at the old Creek town of Tuckabatche (on the Tallapoosa, above Horseshoe Bend), on the night Tecumseh spoke.

Tecumseh, dressed only in a breech-clout, with two crane feathers in his hair, carried a war club painted red as he strode through the Creek warriors.

He had carried his crusade to the Choctaws, in southwest Alabama, but the great Choctaw chief Pushmataha had met him in a sort of Lincoln-Douglas debate. Tecumseh urged war, spill the blood of the white man. But Pushmataha urged peace, the Indian could trust his white brothers. The Choctaws stood by their chief.

Now Tecumseh had come to the Creeks. He would pull them into war with the whites, or his whole mission to the South would fall in failure.

Tecumseh raised his hand, and Menawa's eyes glinted.

"Let the white race perish! They seize your land, they corrupt your women, they trample on the grass of your dead. Back whence they came, upon a trail of blood, they must be driven. Back, back, aye, into the great waters whose accursed waves brought them to our shores.

"Burn their houses, destroy their stock! The red man owns the country and the palefaces must never enjoy it. War now, war forever!"

When Tecumseh finished, the "red sticks" among the Creeks (those favoring war) lifted their voices in great war whoops which shredded the night.

Tecumseh left for Georgia, in a last ditch effort to enlist the Cherokees in his crusade against the whites.

The Creeks argued after he left. Menawa was for war, William McIntosh and other chiefs were for peace. From their arguments before the Creek council, a bitter feud was born between the two chiefs—Menawa and McIntosh. It would last the rest of their lives.

But Menawa and the "red stick" chiefs won out, at least partially. Most of the Creeks declared war against the whites, and blood ran in the forests.

There were scattered skirmishes, then the massacre of whites at Fort Mims in Baldwin County, and the terrified settlers—many of them from Tennessee—called for help from their home state. They called on the governor of Tennessee for help. Gov. William Blount called for volunteers, and appointed Jackson to lead them.

The trail of events led to the fatal loop of the Tallapoosa—Horseshoe Bend—and the American victory. And the power of the Creeks crumbled into dust.

After the battle, Menawa went to his home town of Okfuskee, just down river from Horseshoe Bend on the Tallapoosa. His store had been looted, he had lost his cattle and horses.

Events crowded upon each other. Alabama became a state in 1819, but a large indigestible chunk of Eastern Alabama stuck in its craw—it still belonged to the Creeks, under the treaty signed with Jackson.

In 1791, an Indian agent traveled through the territory of the Creeks and reported that it "must, in process of time, become a most delectable part of the United States."

The territory (parts of Georgia and Alabama) was huge, 84,000 square miles and "remarkably healthy ... the constant breezes, which are probably occasioned by the high hills and numerous rapid watercourses, render the heat of summer very temperate ..."

The Indians may have had treaties with the federal government, but the states—Alabama among them—maintained that the Indians lived in Alabama, and therefore must abide by state laws.

Alabama passed laws banning tribal governments, and placing the Indians under the state government. Some of the laws made it hard for an Indian to testify in court. The Indians appealed for help to Old Mad Jackson, their ancient enemy, now President Andrew Jackson.

Jackson shrugged his shoulders in the White House: nothing he could do about it. The treaties were unenforceable. And he urged the Indians to move beyond the Mississippi, where new land would be given to them.

In 1821 and 1823, William McIntosh of the Creeks made treaties with citizens of Georgia, giving away 15 million acres of Creek land. He had been supported by 12 Creek chiefs, but opposed by 36, representing nine-tenths of the Creek population.

But McIntosh sold the land anyway, taking white money under the table from the Georgia land commissioners. In 1825, McIntosh broke the last straw—he sold another 10 million acres of Creek land.

The opposing Creek chiefs met, and pronounced sentence on McIntosh. He was charged with breaking Creek law, which forbade selling land without the consent of the entire Creek nation.

The penalty: death.

The executioner was Menawa. On May Day of 1825, Menawa led a group of Indian braves to McIntosh's home near Coweta (the present-day site of Phenix City) on the Chattahoochee.

They burned his house, and shot McIntosh to death, killing his son-in-law for good measure.

The 1825 land treaty was annulled, and Menawa went to Washington himself. Here he signed a new treaty, guaranteeing the Creeks that they could hold on to their remaining territory.

As part of the treaty, Menawa held up his right hand and swore allegiance—forever—to the United States of America.

Predictably, the treaty was not quite worth the paper it was written on. By 1831, the Creeks were up against the wall, besieged, reeling from the waves of white squatters. They came from Columbus, Ga., the headquarters for the land-hungry whites who wanted Indian lands, by hook or by crook. Along with the squatters came the bootleggers and the sellers of whiskey.

President Jackson made no bones about it. He said openly he did not intend to enforce the treaties, and he urged the Indians to take the white man's kind offer and "remove"—move themselves to the land west of the Mississippi River.

The situation became heated. Federal troops chased down a man named Hardeman Owens, charged with murdering a U.S. marshal. Owens pulled his pistol, aimed at a soldier, and another soldier shot him dead.

An Alabama grand jury took the side of Owens, who had been active in taking land from the Indians. The jury indicted the soldiers who shot Owens. State law took precedence over the federal law, the state said, and the soldiers would stand trial in state court.

President Jackson sent Francis Scott Key, composer of the *Star Spangled Banner*, to Alabama as an envoy, and Key went along with the state's demands.

Jackson's secretary of war issued orders to U.S. soldiers to remove the Creeks at once, "as a military measure."

There was a second Indian war. A sorrowing Menawa, true to his promise of loyalty to the U.S., joined the army in rounding up the rebellious Creeks, as did nearly 2,000 other Creek warriors.

Menawa cut a sad figure, wearing the uniform of an American general, trying to pacify his grieving Indians.

The captured Indians, called "hostiles" by the military, were started west in a double-file procession, handcuffed and shackled together.

One of them was the 84-year-old Eneah Emathla, who uttered not a word of complaint as he marched off to exile and death.

Earlier, the old chief had told Washington Irving, the writer: "They (the whites) cannot appreciate the feelings of a man that loves his country."

It was a pitiful procession. The Indians took their horses with them, and white thieves lurked around the fringes of the slow-moving procession. They ran off hundreds of Indian horses and cattle.

There were tragedies. Rotten boats sank while crossing the Mississippi, and many Indians were drowned. A cholera epidemic killed hundreds more.

Some of the whites were touched, and some of them snickered in amusement, as the departing Indians—the day before they left for Oklahoma—went about touching leaves, trees, rocks, streams, the land itself—in farewell.

Menawa, old now, a Judas in his general's uniform, had a solid promise from high U.S. authority that he would not have to go.

But this promise too was broken.

On the night before he left for the West, he went back to his old town of Okfuskee on the banks of the Tallapoosa River. He spent the night alone.

To an old white friend the next morning, he said.

"Last evening I saw the sun set for the last time, and its light shine upon the tree tops, and the land, and the water, that I am never to look upon again."

Then he walked away, to join his Creek brethren on the trail to the alien West.

It was a trail of blood and death, countless Indians died of disease and privation along the way.

It was a trail of broken promises, lies, and greed.

It was a trail of exile for 50,000 Indians who were uprooted from the land they loved and sent to a flat alien land in the West.

It was the Trail of Tears.

Eufaula

Chapter Twelve

1836

A tearful farewell To Alabama From an Indian Named Eufaula

The old Indian stood at the speaker's rostrum and looked out on the suspicion, shining darkly in the white faces.

It was one day in 1836, in the House chamber of the State Capitol in Tuscaloosa, and the Indian, Chief Eufaula of the Creeks—had asked for permission to speak to the Alabama Legislature.

Chief Eufaula headed a large band of Creeks who had been forced from their home lands in East Alabama, and now were being forced to march overland to the Indian Territory, present-day Oklahoma.

The old chief held up his right hand, and the hubbub in the legislative hall diminished, and there was silence.

"I come here, brothers, to see the great house of Alabama and the men who make the law," said the old chief, "and to say farewell in brotherly kindliness before I go to the far West, where my people are now going."

Some of the white legislators looked at one another. Are we going to hear that same old song again? Some of them wished he would hurry up and finish, so that uncomfortable feeling would go away.

The band of Creeks had left Coosa County and traveled to Tuscaloosa over the Huntsville Road—women, children, horses, wagons, and their belongings.

Mrs. Clement Clay, wife of an Alabama governor, wrote that the city turned out to see the Indian boys dash through the streets of Tuscaloosa on their ponies. Wrote Mrs. Clay:

"Along the river banks carriages stood, crowded with sightseers watching the squaws as they tossed their young children into the stream in order that they might learn to swim. The belles of the city appeared arrayed in dainty muslins and bonnets in the smartest fashions of the times."

Dr. Joshua Foster, at that time a student at the University of Alabama, visited the Indian camp and bought a few trinkets from them. He saw Indian boys and girls in the Warrior "not clad in modern bathing suits, but all in their birthday suits, or undress uniform, paddling like ducks in the creek."

Back in the House chamber, the old Indian chief stood before the restive legislators. He spoke again.

"In time gone by I have thought that the white men wanted to bring burden and ache of heart upon my people in driving them from their homes and yoking them with laws they did not understand. But I have now become satisfied that they are not unfriendly toward us, but that they wish us well."

Chief Eufaula may have spoken these words with charity in his heart. It seemed to most Indians—in Alabama, in 1836—that the white men "wanted to bring burden and ache of heart" upon them.

With a stroke of a pen in 1813, Gen. Andrew Jackson signed the Treaty of Fort Jackson after the fateful battle of Horseshoe Bend, and ripped away much of the Indian lands in Alabama, opening the state to white settlement.

The Creeks were pushed to a territory east of the Coosa River and the Choctaws were penned west of the Tombigbee. The Cherokees held a pocket in the northeastern corner of the state, and the Chickasaws were ringed into a northwestern corner of the state.

Settlers began to pour into the territory. From only a few thousand, white population jumped to 144,317 in 1820 and to 309,527 in 1830. By the middle 1830s, it was more than 400,000, and land-hungry whites cast greedy eyes on Indian lands that remained.

Treaties were signed—with the Choctaws in 1830, the Creeks in 1832, the Chickasaws in 1834 and the Cherokees in 1835—and they were to last "as long as grass grows or water runs." The Indians were to be paid for their lands and were to be given new lands in the West. The Creeks had an option to stay on in Alabama, to keep part of their lands and stay as citizens.

But even in the face of the treaties, the white settlers simply would not stay out of the Indian territories. Thousands rushed in and dared the Indians—or anybody else—to move them out.

Like feathers from a chicken, the settlers plucked the lands from the Indians. The whites were sorry about the plight of the poor Indians, but their greed overpowered their pity. An editorial in the *Jacksonville Republican* said on May 1, 1838:

"We feel our sympathies rise for them, but they must go; they are bound by treaties so to do; and for the welfare and happiness of this land, they must go to their new homes; the white man and they cannot have the same land..."

But on that day in 1836, staring into the faces of the legislators, Chief Eufaula had tears in his eyes.

"In these lands of Alabama, which have belonged to my forefathers and where their bones lie buried, I see the Indian fires are going out. Soon they will be cold.

"New fires are lighting in the West for us, they say, and we will go there. I do not believe our Great Father means to harm his red children, but that he wishes us well.

"We leave behind our good will to the people of Alabama who will build the great houses and to the men who make the laws. This is all I have to say. I came to speak farewell to the wise men who make the laws and to wish them peace and gladness in the country which my forefathers owned, and which I now part from to go in another home in the West.

"I leave the graves of my fathers, for the Indian fires are almost gone."

The old man ended his speech, and stepped down from the rostrum, and there were some tears in the eyes of the legislators. The old man shook a few hands, left the chamber and walked down the steps of the Capitol, going back to his camp on the river.

In a few days, the Indians gathered their few belongings, hitched their horses to their wagons, and began their lonely trek through Mississippi, Louisiana and Arkansas toward Oklahoma and exile.

Said the *Arkansas Gazette*:

"They presented a most pitiable scene—old men and women, dirty, haggard, and travel-worn from their long journey, drooped their way westward."

Alabama place names
Are Indian heritage

The names, full of clucking consonants and flowing vowels that sound like birds on a mountain stream, crop up across a map of Alabama like chips of living history.

Names of counties, names of cities, names of creeks, even the name of the state itself.

These are the Indian names, flowing down to us from the Creeks, the Choctaws, the Cherokees and the Chickasaws of Alabama's past.

Most of the Indian names came from nature— words that stood for animals, birds, fish, dirt, reptiles, snakes, creeks and rivers, plants, trees, settlements and features of the landscape.

The Creeks, or Muscogees, occupied most of Alabama and Georgia, and their towns lined the rivers— the Alabama, Coosa, Tallapoosa, Flint and Chattahoochee. The Creek tribe of the Alabama (Alabamons, or Alibamos) lived on the Alabama River, just below the junction of the Tallapoosa and the Coosa.

The word *Alabama* comes from the Choctaw word *alba* (plants, weeds) plus *amo* (to cut, to trim, to gather). Thus, *Alabama* means "those who clear the land," or "thicket clearers."

Here are some other Alabama words, uttered by Indians long ago, and where they came from:

Attalla, a city in Etowah County. This Indian place was *Atale*, which is a corruption of the Cherokee word *otali* (mountain).

Autauga, a county in Central Alabama and also a creek which flows into the Alabama River. The name probably comes from the Creek word *atagi*, which means "border."

Cahaba, a river in central Alabama, which flows

into the Alabama River below Selma. Also a town in
Dallas County which served as the state's capital. The
word comes from the Choctaw words *oka* (water) and
aba (above).

Chattahoochee, a river forming the lower boundary between Alabama and Georgia. The word comes
from the Creeks words *chato* (rocks) and *huchi* (marked).
Thus Chattahoochee means "marked rocks."

Chattooga, a river in Cherokee County and north-
west Georgia. It comes from the Cherokee word Tsatugi,
which may mean "I have crossed the stream," from the
Cherokee word *gatsugi* (I have crossed) or *gatugia* (I
sip).

Cherokee, a county in northeast Alabama and a
town in Colbert County. Also the name of the powerful
Indian tribe. It comes from *Tsaragi*, which is an adap-
tation of the Choctaw word *chiluk* (cave). Some Cherokees lived in caves.

Coatopa, a creek and a town in Sumter County.
It comes from the Choctaw *koi* (panther) and *hotupa*
(wounded). Thus *Coatopa* might mean Wounded Panther Creek.

Conecuh, a county and a river in southern Alabama. If the name is Creek, it probably comes from
koha (canebrakes) and *anika* (near). If the name comes
from the Choctaw, it could be from *kuni* (young canes)
and *akka* (below, down there).

Coosa, a river which flows in from Georgia to join
the Tallapoosa River and form the Alabama River. It's
also a county, named for the river. It probably comes
from the Choctaw word *kusha* (cane, or canebrake).

Escambia, a river and a county in southern
Alabama. The name may come from the Choctaw *uski*
(cane) and *amo* (to gather).

Etowah, a county in northern Alabama, where
the city of Gadsden is located. The name probably
comes from a Creek settlement named *itawa*. The word
may come from the Creek word *italwa* (town or tribe).

Talladega, a city and a county in north central Alabama. The name comes from the Creek words *talwa* (town) and *atigi* (border). Talladega mans "border town," and the Creek settlement was near the boundary between the Creeks and the Natchez Indians.

Tallapoosa, a county in east central Alabama, a creek in Clarke County, and a river which joins the Coosa River to form the Alabama River. It probably comes from the Choctaw or Alabama word *tali* (rock) and *pushi* (pulverized).

Tohopeka, a community just south of Horseshoe Bend on the Tallapoosa River. The word comes from the Creek word *tohopki* (fort). The Creeks gave this name to their fort on Horseshoe Bend, which Andrew Jackson destroyed in 1813.

Tombigbee, a river coming out of Mississippi and joining the Alabama about 42 miles north of Mobile to form the Mobile River. The word comes from the Choctaw *itombi* (box) for coffin) and *ikbi* (makes). Thus, Tombigbee means "coffin makers."

Tuscumbia, a city in Colbert County. The name probably came from the Choctaw or Chickasaw *tashka* (warrior) and *umbachi* (rainmaker).

Tuskegee, a town in Macon County. The name probably comes from the Creek word *taskaya* (warrior). In the Alabama dialect, the word for warrior is *taska* and in Choctaw, *tashka*.

Wedowee, a town in central Alabama. There was an Indian village on a creek known as Wahdowwee, near the present town of Wedowee. The name may be a corruption of the Creek *wiwa* (water) and *tawa* (sumac bush).

Weogufka, a creek and a town in Coosa County. It comes from the Creek *wi* (water) and *ogufki* (muddy).

In all, some 231 Indian names have survived in Alabama. Of these, 117 apparently came from the Creeks, and 80 from the Choctaws, with nine from the Cherokees and four from the Chickasaws.

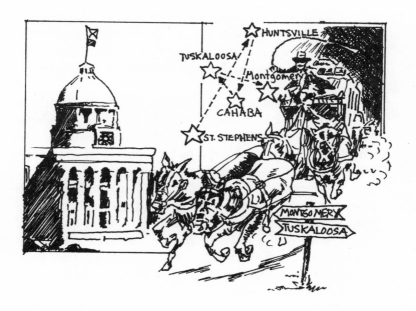

Chapter Thirteen

1846

"Government on wheels" Settles on Goat Hill

The driver cracked his whip over the backs of the galloping horses, and the stagecoach picked up speed, bumping over the dirt road from Selma.

It was after sundown, and the driver squinted in the early darkness, trying to see the road. Then the lights of Montgomery came into view over a low hill, and the driver cracked his whip again.

Downtown, there was a clump of people waiting, and the driver yelled at them as he pulled the stagecoach to a creaking stop.

"They did it! They did it! They moved the capital

to Montgomery!"

A cheer burst from the crowd, and somebody went running to the hotel lobbies and taverns to spread the news. More cheers, and glasses were raised in the streets.

It was the evening of Jan. 30, 1846, and the good news was: The Alabama Legislature, meeting at the capitol in Tuskaloosa (that's how they spelled the city then, after the great Indian warrior) had voted to move the capital to Montgomery.

One historian says: "The people of Montgomery proceeded to celebrate the event by a grand jollification." And a grand jollification it must have been, because the people of Montgomery and Alabama's Black Belt had been trying to snare the capital away from Tuskaloosa for 20 years.

Andrew Dexter, the founder of Montgomery, had forecast that it would become the state's capital one day, and now Dexter's dream had come true.

And that night, as the "jollification" spread downtown among the flickering streets lights, people raised their glasses up the long street named for Dexter, toward the dark mound of earth at the head of the street: Goat Hill, where cattle and goats grazed and where the new capitol would stand.

For the first 27 years of its life, Alabama had what some called a "government on wheels," moving from one place to another.

One year at St. Stephens, above the white limestone bluff on the Alabama River in Washington County. Another year at Huntsville on the Tennessee. Six years in the freshly built city of Cahaba, in Dallas County, where the Cahaba flows into the Alabama. Then 20 years in Tuskaloosa on the Warrior River.

For almost 30 of Alabama's beginning years, the location of the capital was the burning political question of the day.

It was a contest, really, between the river systems

of the state—the Alabama in the east, the Tombigbee in the west, and the Tennessee in the north.

The people living in these river basins wanted the capital in their area, and for good reason.

In the fight to remove the capitol from Tuskaloosa in 1845-46, *The Montgomery Advertiser* editorialized:

"There is not a man who owns a house and lot in this city, or within a mile of it, who is not directly and immediately interested. The man who owns land will have its value enhanced, and everyone who sells lumber, corn, meal, beef, vegetables, turkeys, chickens, milk, butter, eggs, beef, mutton, pork, or articles of any kind consumed in cities will have the prospect of an enlarged market and increased consumption. Let us therefore unite and work together to accomplish that in which we are all interested."

The people of Tuskaloosa, or of course, didn't want to lose the capital. It would be like putting the capital on wheels, they said.

"The spectacle will be presented of fifty wagons, at every adjournment of the Legislature, moving off with the archives...to a place agreed upon by the majority...(the people of each area) taking their turn at the seat of government."

The contest began in 1818, when Gov. William Wyatt Bibb (a former Georgian) reported to the second session of the Alabama Territorial Legislature in St. Stephens, meeting in rooms of the Douglass Hotel.

A legislative committee had recommended Tuskaloosa, but Bibb ignored the report.

Instead, he broke the news to the Legislature. He had a grant of land from the federal government for 1620 acres of land at Cahaba, in Dallas County, on the Alabama River.

Free land for a capital city, and they could sell lots and raise money for the capitol building itself.

It was a political stroke, for the treasury of the new territory/state of Alabama was almost bare, and the Legislature went along with the governor.

A year of temporary quarters in Huntsville, waiting for the capitol building to be finished in Cahaba, and the new government loaded up its papers again, moving from Huntsville to Cahaba in November of 1820.

Gov. Bibb had pulled a political coup on locating the capital at Cahaba, but now the river defeated him. The town was located in the last horseshoe curve of the Cahaba River before it joined the Alabama.

In high water, the Alabama acted as a dam on the waters of the Cahaba, backing them up, and it overflowed its banks into the new town.

Toward the end, the floods became so bad the legislators had to row back and forth from their hotels to the capitol in skiffs. Tuskaloosa men in the Legislature wrote a report, blasting Cahaba as the seat of government.

A Jefferson County senator played a crucial part in removing the capitol from Cahaba to Tuskaloosa in 1826.

The senator, John (Red) Brown, favored moving to Tuskaloosa. He beat out a man named John Wood, and Wood contested the election.

The Tuskaloosa legislators knew where Brown stood, and they weren't sure of Wood, so they supported Brown for the seat, and he won the election contest— and supported Tuskaloosa.

Sure enough, the vote to remove the capitol from Cahaba to Tuskaloosa was close—11 to 10 in the Senate—and Brown was the deciding vote.

More wagons, more carting of state records, on the road to Tuskaloosa. Here, a state capitol was built, and it stayed put for 20 years.

But things were changing. Population and wealth were building up in East Alabama, and things came to a head again in 1846.

Lobbyists flooded to the Legislature, extolling the

virtues of their area, offering deals, trying to tie the vote down. Montgomery, Selma, Wetumpka and Mobile all hoped the capital city lightning would strike them.

The *Tuskaloosa Monitor*, a newspaper, editorialized:

"Ten miles (beyond Selma) is a place of bats and owls, known 20 years ago as the seat of government. High water overflows it, and the old State House was actually washed down by inundation. That place, so deserted and lonely, has screwed itself up in the chorus for removal...Cahaba wants it for the pleasure of running skiffs under the windows of the capitol to save members from drowning in their seats when the Alabama River spreads itself."

The *Monitor* conceded that Montgomery was a growing city, but "wagons, drays and auctions, the fruit of active commerce, like that of Montgomery, would not detract the minds of the members of the Legislature."

In 1846, the contest in the Legislature came to white heat.

On Jan. 28, 1846, the legislators trooped from their hotels, down the streets of Tuskaloosa, and into the capitol. Today, they would decide.

Placed in nomination were Tuskaloosa, Wetumpka, Mobile, Montgomery, Statesville, Selma, Marion, and Huntsville.

On the first ballot, the vote was Tuskaloosa 39, Montgomery 33, Wetumpka 28, Selma 9, Huntsville 6, Mobile 6, Marion 4, and Statesville 2.

One can almost see them, the Alabama River boys from Montgomery, Wetumpka and Selma, whispering and nodding in one corner of the House chamber.

Look, they must have whispered to each other, if we get our votes together, we can move it to the banks of the Alabama—somewhere on the Alabama.

And they did get together. On the 16th ballot, the capital was moved. Montgomery received 68 votes, a majority, against Tuskaloosa's 39 votes. And the

Speaker of the House rapped his gavel: Montgomery will be the new capital.

Downtown, at the depot, the driver lashed his horses, armed with news he was to take to Montgomery.

Later, the government on wheels rolled for the last time. State archives were packed into 113 boxes, which were loaded onto 13 wagons, and the governmental wagon train set out for Montgomery.

The Montgomery City Council quickly passed a bond issue, borrowing $75,000 to build the new capitol building, and the deed to Goat Hill passed to the state. The new capitol was built, and the government moved in. The first legislative session in the new statehouse began in December of 1847.

With the move, the Black Belt and east central Alabama became the center of Alabama politics.

The "Georgia boys"—the settlers from Georgia who had settled along the Alabama River, had wrested control from the "Tennessee boys," settlers from Tennessee who had come down to settle along the Tennessee River and the Warrior-Tombigbee.

The "Georgia boys" stood with Sen. John C. Calhoun of South Carolina: they were the states' rights advocates, the ones who yelled the loudest that states' rights outweighed federal law.

The "Tennessee boys" from Tennessee and North Carolina, were Andrew Jackson people, hard-core unionists.

Locating the capital on the Alabama River had an obvious advantage: it was easier for legislators from the Alabama River to get to the capital. For those in the Tennessee Valley and along the Warrior-Tombigbee, a trip to the capital could take days, sometimes weeks.

The split showed in the Alabama secession convention of 1861, when the Alabama River people voted to leave the Union. And the Tennessee-Tombigbee-Warrior people voted to stay in the Union. Here again, the Black Belt-Alabama River section won out, and Alabama left the Union.

The move to Montgomery in 1846 and 1847 seemed to stop the wheels of Alabama's rolling government.

But in December 1849, the Legislature was sitting in the new statehouse on Goat Hill. A Mr. Blevins of Dallas County was pushing a resolution that slaves should be counted to determine representation in the Legislature, even though they couldn't vote.

Then somebody smelled smoke.

The capitol was on fire, the roof of the House of Representatives was burning. It was written into the House journal:

"Note by the clerk: Pending the above motion, at one o'clock and fifteen minutes p.m., an alarm of fire was given. The roof of the capitol was discovered to be in flames, and in three hours from the first alarm the broken walls alone remained."

Next day, the Senate met in the saloon of the Montgomery Hall, a famous hotel of the day, and the House of Representatives met in the hotel's ballroom.

The question arose: Shall we rebuild in Montgomery, or move again? A Wilcox County legislator tried to move the capital to Mobile, temporarily, of course. A Morgan County legislator tried to amend the resolution to move the statehouse back to Tuskaloosa.

But the legislators voted to stay in Montgomery, and a new capitol, the present building, was built.

And here it stayed, even serving as the capital of the Confederacy, until the seat of government was moved to Richmond, so the leaders could be closer to the war.

But hope springs eternal. When Birmingham was founded early in 1870s, a park was dedicated at 20th Street downtown.

It's called Linn Park now. Before that, it was Woodrow Wilson Park.

But its first name, in expectation that the capital would be moved to Birmingham?

They called it Capital Park.

Chapter Fourteen

1854

———

For a moment In history, Steamboat is king Of Alabama's rivers

From a satellite, tracing its 100-mile-high orbit in ghostly silence, they look like shining snakes. Writhing, twisting, coiling, slicing the land, they move to the south, to the calm blue bowl of the Gulf of Mexico.

The rivers of Alabama.

Blink your eyes, imagine another time, and you can see the movement out of the woods, a herd of white-

*tailed deer coming down to the water's edge to get a
drink. You can see Indian canoes, sliding gently down
the broad muddy highways. And then, in another blink,
the smoke and bustle and whistle of the steamboat,
pulling up to a small town landing, like a circus come
to town.*

*Blink your eyes again, to now, and you can see the
gigantic eight-barge tows, with the squat, muscular
tugboat behind them, pushing upstream.*

The rivers of Alabama.

****

Rumble...rumble...rumble...BOOM!

The great steamboat rested at the landing, gently
breathing steam, at the bottom of the tall bluff, and the
cotton bales skidded crazily down the wooden chute,
like runaway children on a slide.

The bales careened onto the deck and crashed into
bales with a hollow BOOM, and quickly the black men,
backs glistening with sweat, snagged them with their
hooks and wrestled them into place on the deck.

Over it all, outlining the figures in flickering light,
were the flares. The pine knots burned at the top of the
hill, where the "rolladores" pushed the bales over the
cliff, down the slide. And the flares burned like bright
flags along the deck of the steamboat.

Some of the passengers came on the high Texas
deck and leaned against the rail, watching the cotton
bales slam aboard.

A man named Charles Lanman, writing in 1858,
described the scene:

"The whole aspect of an Alabama bluff when a
steamer is shipping cotton at night is truly beautiful,
for then it is that pitch-pine torches illuminate the
entire scene, and, while the gay passengers are dancing and feasting in the gilded saloon of the steamer, the
loud and plaintive singing of the Negroes give anima-

tion and cheerfulness to all whose lot is to toil.

"In managing the heavy bales the Negroes invariably work in pairs, and an iron hook, which each man always carries about his person, is the unmistakable badge of his profession."

Early the next morning, riding low in the water with its decks piled high with hundreds of bales of cotton, the steamboat backed away from the landing and headed downstream for Mobile.

On its way down the Alabama River, the steamboat passed other steamboats moving upstream toward Montgomery and Wetumpka, and they serenaded each other with shrill songs from their steam calliopes, and the people waved hello, goodbye.

During most of the 19th century, from about 1820 on, the rivers of Alabama—the Tombigbee, the Alabama, the Black Warrior, the Tennessee, the Tallapoosa, the Coosa, the Chattahoochee—were the highways of the state.

Most freight, and most passengers, moved from one place to another on the rivers.

Towns sprang up along the water—St. Stephens, Demopolis, Tuscaloosa, Selma, Cahaba, Montgomery, Huntsville, Decatur—and the river traffic sustained them.

It was a big event, a spectacle, when a huge steamboat rounded the bed and huffed its way toward the landing.

Bells rang, little boys raced down the streets toward the wharf, and people went down to see who and what had arrived.

Downriver, heading for Mobile, it was mostly cotton, bales piled high around the deck. Upriver, the steamboats carried manufactured goods from Eastern cities, and goods shipped from Europe, plus tropical fruits and other goods from South America.

Before 1820, before the steamboats came to the Alabama rivers, there were flatboats, then keelboats.

In the early days, boatmen would build a flatboat, load it with cotton, and float it downriver for Mobile. At the port, they would unload the cotton and dismantle their boat, selling the wood for lumber.

Then it was the long trip back upstate. Sometimes they walked back, sometimes they rode horses.

When the keelboats came, the boatmen would float their cargo downstream, then embark on the backbreaking task of wrestling the boat upstream.

Carefully staying out of the mid-channel current, the boatmen poled their boat along the bank. Sometimes they hoisted sails when the wind sprang up, sometimes they hooked trees and bushes with their poles, and pulled the boat upstream. Sometimes the boatmen went ashore and pulled the boat by ropes, even using a pulley against strong current.

The first steamboat built in the state was the *Alabama*, completed in 1818 at St. Stephens. The *Tensas* was built in 1819 in Blakeley, and it worked the Tombigbee, going up as far as Demopolis.

Oct. 22, 1821, was a great day in the history of Alabama river travel. That day the steamboat *Harriet* arrived in Montgomery after a speedy 10-day trip from Mobile. In the days of keelboat travel, the trip took weeks or months.

People cheered on the Montgomery dock, whistles tooted, and a new day of river travel was born.

The head of navigation on the Alabama River was Wetumpka, just up from Montgomery. During the dry season, steamboats could only go on the Tombigbee as far as Demopolis, but during the wet season, with the rivers high, boats could go all the way up to Cotton Gin Port, in Mississippi.

The Tennessee River was a different story. The people there sent their cotton and other cargo down the Tennessee—up into Tennessee and Kentucky to the Ohio, and down the Mississippi to New Orleans.

On their way up and down the rivers of Alabama,

the steamboats had "filling stations," or fueling places along the way. A steamboat captain would contract with a plantation owner to stack up fuel—cords of wood—at a certain place on the bank.

Then the boat would sweep into the landing, take on the wood, and steam off down the river.

Depending on the way you traveled, passage of a steamboat could be comfortable—or fairly primitive. Going first class, you could stay in a sumptuous cabin, eat off damask tablecloths with silver cutlery, and dance in the grand saloon to the music of a string band.

But if you were a deck passenger, you curled up on a cotton bale to sleep, and you ate what food you brought in your knapsack.

There were accidents—some steamboats blew up with a bang that resounded up and down the river, when their steam boilers overloaded and exploded. Others sank, punctured by a hidden snag in the river, or clutched in a deadly embrace by a sandbar. Some, like the *Eliza Battle* on the Tombigbee, caught fire and burned.

There were steamboat races when owners got their gambling blood up. Here is an account by a man named Thomas D. DeLeon.

"There is a sharp click of our pilot's bell, a gasping throb, as if our boat took a deep long breath. The *Senator* (the other boat in the race) follows in gallant style—both engines roaring and snorting like angry hippopotami—both vessels rocking and straining 'til they seem to paw their way through the churned water.

"Foot by foot, we gain steadily until the gap is widened to three or four boat lengths. (Then the rival boat catches up, and passes.)

"Close down to the water's edge—scarce above the line of foam she cuts—her lower deck lies black and undefined in the shadow of the great mass above it. Suddenly it lights up with a lurid flash, as the furnace doors spring wide open and in the hot glare, the Negro stokers—their stalwart forms jetty black, naked to the waist and streaming with exertion that makes the muscles strain out in great cords—show like the distorted imps of some pictured inferno.

"Little by little—so little we test it by counting her windows—we reach her wheel—pass and lock her bow, and run nose and nose for a hundred feet.

"The stillness of death is upon both boats; not a sound but the creak and shudder as they struggle on. Suddenly the hard voice of our old pilot crashed through it like broadaxe:

"'Goodbye, Sen'tor (the other boat), I'll send yer a tug,' and he gives his bell a merry click.

"Our huge boat gives one shuddering throb that racks her from end to end—one plunge—and then she settles into a steady rush and forges rapidly and evenly ahead."

Some of the steamboat men were colorful, others were downright mean.

There was Bob Otis, a good riverboat captain but a bad apple.

Look at him cross-eyed in a Mobile bar, make a slurring remark about his small size, and you'd find yourself in the alley, trying to dodge his flashing knife.

One day in the mid-1850s, Bob Otis stood on the Texas deck of the *St. Charles*, tethered to the Dauphin Street dock in Mobile. He glowered at another riverboat docked nearby.

Crewmen from the *St. Charles* heard crewmen from the other boat, the *F.P. Kimball*, say they could outrun the *St. Charles* to Montgomery.

The arguments became bar fights, and the bar fights became a glowing feud. Finally, the race was on, and the boats shoved off in the evening, in flurry of swirling smoke and ringing bells. A dockside crowd watched them smoke into the distance and disappear.

As the sun came up the next day, the two boats were nearing Claiborne, a bustling river port in Monroe County. The *Kimball* was in the lead, but the *St. Charles* was closing.

The diminutive Otis stood by the pilothouse, staring at the rival boat.

The *St. Charles* edged alongside the *Kimball*, every muscle straining to pass. Suddenly the *Kimball* veered and its bow bumped the *St. Charles* aft.

The *St. Charles* was pushed toward the bank but recovered. Otis raced to his cabin and came out with a gun. He leveled the rifle at the *Kimball* pilot house and pulled the trigger. The *Kimball* pilot Walter Tuggle, slumped over the wheel, with a bullet wound under his eye.

Now, with the wheel spinning in the pilot house, the *Kimball* veered toward the bank. Captain Greer rushed into the pilothouse and straightened out his boat. As he steered, he shouted curses toward Otis, standing by the pilot house, still holding the gun.

The law took over. Otis was arrested and returned by first boat to Mobile. From there, he came back to Monroeville, where he made bond on a charge of assault with intent to commit murder.

Tuggle recovered. Otis stood trial. The jury found him guilty of assault with a weapon, and the judge put a heavy fine on him—but no jail time.

Obviously the Monroe County judge didn't like a riverboat ramming another in the middle of a race.

Little Captain Bob then changed his ways. He married a Miss Booth, and a reporter wrote:

"Under her gentle influence he became a converted man, and when he laid down his captain's baton he was as good a man as his older brother..."

But the primal tug of the river was too much. Otis invested his life savings into a little riverboat. A reporter wrote:

"I do not suppose Bob Otis ever told a lie or deceived a friend, (but he) died poor—having lost his all in the wreck of a small stern-wheel steamer..."

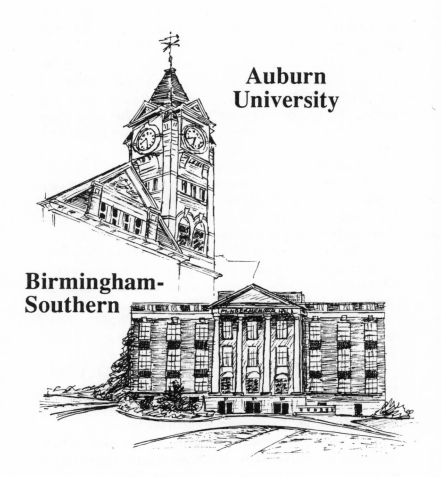

Auburn University

Birmingham-Southern

Chapter Fifteen

1854

Archaelaus spoke, And two colleges Were born

When Archaelaus H. Mitchell stood up to speak at the Alabama Methodist Conference in 1854, Birmingham-Southern College and Auburn University were born.

As Methodists from all over Alabama listened, Mitchell came down hard on eastern universities such as Harvard and Yale.

Their philosophies were suspect. And at the state universities, there was "perpetual strife along the different religious denominations for supremacy." And on Presbyterian college campuses, he said students were fed "on the husks of Calvinism."

What we need, he said in no uncertain terms, is a *Methodist* college in Alabama. LaGrange College, in the hills of Franklin County was a Methodist College, founded in 1830. But planters and preachers from the Black Belt said it was too far away.

Mitchell's speech struck a spark: The Methodist Conference passed a resolution. Any city or town which raised $100,000 for a college would get a school, backed by the Methodists.

Auburn and Greensboro were the front-runners in the race, and the rivalry was bitter. The editor of the *Auburn Gazette* said that Greensboro, which had no railroad, was remote and inaccessible.

Not only that, he wrote, but Greensboro had just recently passed new laws against drunkenness, profanity and fighting in the streets. And, he smirked in print, in his many years as a resident, he had never seen any drunkenness, heard no swearing, and had seen no fights in Auburn.

The editor of the *Greensboro Beacon* struck back in kind. Sure, he wrote, Greensboro was not on a railroad like Auburn, but that was an advantage. Railroads brought to a town "adventurers, loafers, pickpockets and rowdies."

As the Methodist Conference of 1855, the race was a tie. Both communities had come in with pledges of more than $100,000.

During the debate, one minister denounced the people of Auburn as "paupers." The Auburn delegation, stung at the insult, withdrew their offer. But they had no idea of giving up.

On Feb. 1, 1856, one week after Southern University was chartered in Greensboro as a Methodist institution, the Alabama Legislature passed a bill over the governor's veto. It was an act incorporating the East

Alabama Male College in Auburn. The Methodist Conference took over the college in 1859.

The two schools, born in a speech at a Methodist Conference, went their separate ways.

In Greensboro, the Southern University first opened its doors to students on Oct. 3, 1859, with an enrollment of 52 students. The school limped through the Civil War at half strength or less, then picked up steam after the war.

In the beginning Southern University was for men only. But in 1868, Julia Tutwiler knocked on the doors for admission. She filed with the faculty a paper advocating "the admission of females to the classes of male college on the same footing with males."

William May Wightman, a native of South Carolina who had taught at Randolph-Macon and had been president of Wofford College, found the request "novel and startling." But on his recommendation, the trustees allowed Julia Tutwiler to attend classes. By 1897, Southern University was officially co-ed. The first woman graduate was Margaret Pickett, a niece of Julia Tutwiler.

In 1916, The Southern University merged with Birmingham College to become Birmingham-Southern College.

Birmingham-Southern, on Birmingham's westside, has become a topflight school, consistently rated among the top small colleges in the nation.

In Auburn, the East Alabama Male College opened on Oct. 1, 1859, under the presidency of the Rev. William Jeremiah Sasnett, with five teachers and an enrollment of 80 students and 113 students in the preparatory department.

War came in 1861, and the students volunteered to fight with the Confederates. The school closed down until 1866, and struggled through the late 1860s.

In 1868, Alabama accepted the land grant available from the federal government for education. The state sold 240,000 acres of land, raising $253,500 for operation of a school. The Methodist Conference had a building, but no operating funds, so the conference gave the building to the State of Alabama.

On Feb. 26, 1872, the school became the Agricultural and Mechanical College of Alabama, the first land grant college set up in the South separate from a state university. The land grant idea was to make education available to working classes of Americans, instead of restricting college education to the rich.

The change from a classical college to a new technical scientific school was hard. Dr. William Leroy Broun stressed the South's great need for scientific education, and advocated teaching more science.

The board resisted his ideas, and he resigned, going to the University of Texas. The new president, Col. David French Boyd, had been president of Louisiana State University. He pushed the same ideas of scientific education, and the board backed him. But Boyd left for LSU, his first love, and Dr. Broun was brought back from Texas, which must have been a sweet trip for him.

Dr. Broun established a manual training laboratory, an electrical engineering unit, and a first class biological laboratory. Also, first in Alabama, he bought women to the school as students in 1892.

That same year, Auburn entered intercollegiate football with a solid 10-0 win over Georgia.

In 1899, the school became the Alabama Polytechnic Institute. Dr. Luther Noble Duncan became president in 1935, and he established the Cooperative Extension Service and the Engineering Extension Service.

The greatest growth of the school came after World War II, under the leadership of Dr. Ralph Brown Draughon, who served from 1947 until 1965.

In 1960, the name was changed to Auburn University.

Dr. Harry M. Philpott, who became president in 1965, continued the building boom. A Fine Arts Center was built, along with sports complex for intramural and intercollegiate athletics. A 3,000-acre center for agricultural research was set up in Macon County, and two new schools—business and nursing—were established.

Throughout its history, people had tried to define "the Auburn spirit," the thing that makes Auburn different from other schools.

Burns Bennett, a newspaper columnist, tried to explain it this way during a commencement speech:

"Nowhere else do you feel the warmth and *esprit de corps* evinced on The Plains, from the president down to the lowliest freshman with his perpetual 'Hey!'

"No one's a stranger at Auburn. Auburn is hard to explain. Auburn men never let other Auburn men down. There's little class distinction. If you say 'He's an Auburn man,' that seems to be all that's necessary. They don't explain, 'He's rich,' or 'He's poor,' that he's a company president or a clerk. The fact that he's an Auburn man is enough."

****

A small postscript
How Auburn Got Its Name:

It was 1836, and Judge John J. Harper and his son Thomas headed eastward toward Georgia in their buggy.

Behind them lay the raw new buildings of the small Alabama town near the Georgia line. Judge Harper had come to Alabama and helped build the little town; now he and his son were going back to Georgia to get their family and slaves.

At young Tom's suggestion, they stopped at the home of a Mr. Taylor, where they had stayed on their way to Alabama. The young man had not forgotten the beautiful 15-year-old girl, Lizzie Taylor.

Tom Harper and Lizzie Taylor sat on the porch and talked. Tom told her about the little town back in Alabama that he and his father had helped to build.

"Our new town has no name. Won't you propose one?"

"Auburn!" she clapped her hands. "name it Auburn. 'Sweet Auburn, loveliest village of the plain.'" She remembered the quote from Oliver Goldsmith.

The next year, two things happened. The young couple's friendship ripened into love, and they were married.

And when it came time to name the new town, there were two names proposed: Geneva and Auburn. Someone held a long straw and a short one in their fist, and the Auburn straw was pulled out.

The town's name—and later the name of a great university—was Auburn.

"No one's a stranger at Auburn. Auburn is hard to explain. Auburn men never let other Auburn men down. There's little class distinction. If you say, 'He's an Auburn man,' that seems to be all that's necessary."

—Burns Bennett

Chapter Sixteen

1858

——————

Love and death
On the flaming river

The pilot, Daniel Eppes, was worried. He looked down from the pilot house and heard the slaves singing, as cold as it was. It was a mournful sound.

The black men manhandled the cotton bales from the landing onto the main deck of the steamboat. One on top of another, the bales climbed higher, all around the main. The steamboat looked like a fortress of cotton bales.

Eppes turned and looked out at the river. The heavy rains had pushed it up and out of its banks, and it reached, flat and brown and swift, out through the trees of the bottomland.

To some, it looked like a muddy pond, but Eppes saw the ruthless muscle of the current, saw the white plumes, the rooster tails, flaring against the trees.

Eppes knew this river like the back of his hand. But the rising waters had browned out many of the landmarks he knew. The rippling water of a bluff shoal here, the swirling water of a submerged snag there— all gone, buried under the brown flood.

He thought of the Choctaw name for the river— Itomba Igaby, the box maker's creek. The white men had taken the name of a creek which flowed into the river, and named the river for the creek.

Tombigbee, the white men called it. The Indians had called the creek Itomba Igaby after an Indian who built coffins. Eppes shivered, either from the cold or thoughts of the Indian who made coffins.

The door to the pilot house opened, and Capt. S. G. Stone came inside, quickly shutting the door behind him. Eppes tucked his cloak high around his neck as the blast of cold air swept through the pilot house.

He turned to the captain, and shook his head. "We may be getting overloaded, captain," he said. No, said Stone, the *Eliza Battle* is a good stout boat, we can carry the load all right.

The packet, weighing 325 tons, was built in New Albany, Ind., in 1852. She was the new queen of the "Bigbee" river trade, carrying freight and passengers upriver from Mobile, and cotton and passengers down river from Aberdeen and Columbus, Miss.

She was named for a member of a famous Mobile family, as was the hotel, The Battle House.

Two days before, the Eliza Battle had taken on cotton and passengers at Columbus, Miss. There were more stops on the way down to Demopolis, stops for wood, stops for more cotton, a landing to take on passengers.

Now the *Eliza Battle* had pulled into a landing at

Warsaw, in Sumter County, between Demopolis and Myrtlewood. It sat there, wisps of smoke fleecing from the tall red chimneys forward, as the black men wrestled the cotton aboard.

Down below at the gangplank, 18-year-old Frank Stone—the boat's second clerk and the son of the captain—checked the cotton and passengers.

He watched, list in hand, as a carriage swept up to the landing, and a young couple climbed out. Other people on the landing cheered and some of them threw rice. It was Mary Taylor and her handsome new husband, just married at the Taylor mansion up on the hill.

Samuel Taylor, the planter, came to Alabama from South Carolina in the 1840s. He had put together a great plantation on the Tombigbee with scores of slaves, many fine mules and a great house on the hill.

When it was ready to pick, Taylor's cotton stretched out across the bottomland like snow.

Taylor and his wife had one daughter, Mary, the belle of the county. She and a boy from a neighboring plantation, Philip Saunders, had grown up as childhood sweethearts.

Philip had proposed to her in the parlor of the Taylor mansion, and she had taken his ring, and the plantation prepared for a wedding.

Then, the story goes, along came a handsome stranger, and swept Mary Taylor off her feet. She handed the ring back to Philip Saunders and married the stranger.

They had been married this day—Feb. 28, 1858— and now they came across the gangplank onto the *Eliza Battle,* on their honeymoon trip to Mobile and Mardi Gras.

Saunders was heartbroken, but curiously, he was not bitter. From his face, from the way he looked at her, anyone could tell he still loved Mary Taylor, that he would always love her.

Philip Saunders boarded the boat too, headed for

Mobile and a lonely Mardi Gras.

The cotton was loaded, the passengers were aboard, and young Frank Stone ordered up the gangplank. Daniel Eppes barked his orders, and the great sidewheels began to slosh backwards in the water.

The *Eliza Battle* backed into the muddy stream, then the wheels stopped, and began to move forward. The boat picked up speed and moved downstream.

Night came on the river, and there was sleet, mixed with snow, slanting across the deck. Eppes, up in the pilot house, strained his eyes. As he rounded a bend, he felt a touch of panic—the Eliza Battle was overloaded, and it felt heavy, sluggish. But he calmly gave the great wheel an extra half turn, right foot resting on the bottom rung, and the boat hesitated, then swung around the bend.

It was a strange contrast—Eppes looked out on the snow and sleet and the dangerous black water, while below him, in the ballroom with flickering lamps, there was music and laughter.

In the ballroom, Saunders watched Mary Taylor and her new husband promenade down the floor. The knife of pain cut deeper as he saw the love in her face when she looked up at him.

With the aid of whiskey slipped to them by the passengers, the black musicians were having a fine old time. They played a new song, "Way Down Upon the Sewanee River," and the passengers clapped and cheered. More, more.

There was a blast from the Eliza Battle's steam whistle, and the passengers bundled up and came outside, lining the rail on the port side. Heading upstream, bravely moving against the sullen brown water, was another steamer, coming up from Mobile.

There were cheers as the two boats passed each other, and the *Eliza Battle's* steam calliope played "Annie Laurie." The other calliope answered, and the boats serenaded each other with shrill steam music in the dark night.

As the boat passed, sparks erupted from the twin chimneys of the other boat, and some of them settled onto the cotton bales near the stern of the *Eliza Battle*. The sparks smoldered among the hard-packed bales.

In the ballroom, there was the bouncy music: "Alabama girls, won't you come out tonight...come out tonight...come out tonight...Alabama girls, won't you come out tonight...and dance by the light of the moon."

People were clapping their hands and singing. John Powell, the bartender from Mobile, was busy, pouring one drink after another.

A spark in a cotton bale near the stern grew into a small flame. It burned, and grew, and licked upward to the bale above it, and the fire flared.

In the pilot house, Eppes squinted against the darkness ahead, trying to read the river. The channel was hard to follow in the darkness, and once he felt the gentle tug of mud. Again, he panicked, but concealed it well, and he swung the wheel quickly, and he felt the mud hold on, then release the boat.

Then came the cry which froze Eppes backbone: FIRE!

Eppes walked to the rear of the pilot house and looked aft. He could see the men outlined against the flames, beating at the fire. He sent word for the captain, and Stone appeared in the doorway of the pilot house, his face white with fear.

It was after midnight, and the snow and sleet flitted across the deck. Stone looked at the fire, then climbed down the ladder and walked to the doorway of the ballroom.

Inside, there was the music and bright laughter. Stone, his face hard, stepped inside. The faces turned to him in smiles, then turned fearful as he held up his hand.

"Ladies and gentlemen, the boat is on fire," said Stone, and a woman screamed. He held up his hand again, trying to warn against panic, but there were more screams, and the passengers swept past him, out onto the deck. At the stern, the fire burned brightly now, throwing a circle of firelight on the brown water aft.

There was a rush for lifeboats. Some say there were no lifeboats aboard, others say the fire made it impossible to launch the lifeboats. In any event, there were no lifeboats available.

The fire moved forward along the cotton bales on deck, out of control now. Some of the passengers bound pieces of lumber together, trying to make rafts, and pushed them out into the darkness.

Others pushed cotton bales over the side, and tried to ride them ashore. But there was no shore, the water stretched for hundreds of yards into the surrounding countryside.

In the pilot house, Capt. Stone ordered Pilot Eppes to drive the *Eliza Battle* into the bank. But the tiller ropes were burned through, and the boat careened crazily down the river, spinning, turning, crunching over trees, bumping into snags, lurching into a bend, then drifting back into the channel.

As the fire crowded the passengers into the bow, some jumped into the freezing water. Others clung to the burning boat and hoped it would touch the bank so they could jump off.

Berrien Cromwell of Sumter, called Bat by his friends, looked wildly around the deck. He caught his wife by the arm, and hurried to their cabin. They woke their small son, and snatched up their baby, and rushed back into the deck.

The son became separated from them in the melee, and Cromwell and his wife and baby climbed into a tree as the *Eliza Battle* brushed through the flooded woods.

Frank Stone, the 18-year second clerk, saved Cromwell's young son, taking him to dry ground. Then he swam back to the burning boat, and rescued a girl named Sallie Turner, pushing her ahead of him on a cotton bale.

He reached safety with her, and she thanked him for saving her life. Then she pleaded: "Oh, please, save my mother and my sister."

For the third time, Frank Stone swam back through the freezing water and climbed aboard the boat. He found Miss Turner's sister and swam with her to high ground, but she later died of exposure. The mother had climbed into a tree. She died during the night.

Cromwell and his wife and baby sat in the tree and watched the boat burn. Toward morning, Cromwell cried as he felt his wife drop away from life. She and the baby died as he held them in his arms.

During the panic, Philip Saunders stood on the deck near his beloved Mary Taylor and her husband. He watched as they held hands and jumped together over the side.

A pull stronger than life made Saunders jump into the swirling brown water with them.

In the light of the flaming boat, he saw Mary Taylor come up. She looked around for her husband and screamed. But he was gone.

Saunders swam to her, and caught her as she was sinking. He swam with her to a clump of trees nearby, and pulled her upwards into the low-lying branches. She was unconscious now, and he held her in his arms, trying to warm her with his love.

Later, when the boats came, he yelled for help and soon a skiff angled against the current, bringing blankets and warmth and safety.

The glare from the burning boat was a fire alarm for the people of Naheola, a landing just downstream, and they came in boats to help. Planters from nearby plantations aroused their slaves and quickly built rafts to join in the rescue efforts.

Dawn came, the snow and sleet continued to fall,

and the blackened hulk of the Eliza Battle sank. Rescuers picked survivors out of trees, and took them to the riverside plantation of Mrs. Rebecca Coleman Pettigrew.

Here, the big house and all the outbuildings became hospitals. The survivors huddled around huge bonfires, trying to keep warm. Huge washpots of soup were ladled up to fight the chill. At one time, there were 75 people recovering at the Pettigrew place.

For almost a week, Mrs. Pettigrew and her family and servants cared for the people of the *Eliza Battle*. Then the families came to comfort their living and bury their dead. Men in rowboats gathered bodies for days afterwards from the brush on the shore.

There is no exact figure for the dead. Some say 29, others say more than 50. The carpenters from the neighboring plantations spent their time making coffins.

For the moment, the Tombigbee was truly the Itomba Igaby, the box maker's creek.

Most historians believe a spark from the other steamer's chimneys lit the fatal fire.

But some 30 years after the tragedy, an Irishman in New York—on his deathbed—told a story of a robbery on the *Eliza Battle* just before the fire broke out.

He and a companion set fire to the boat, he said, to cover their crime. Most historians give little credence to the dying Irishman's story.

At the Pettigrew home, Philip Saunders nursed Mary Taylor. She lingered for a while between life and death, now and then crying in the night. Saunders sat by her bedside, feeding her soup, and praying for her life.

Mary Taylor lived, and went back upstream to her plantation home in Warsaw. Shortly afterwards, her parents died, and she became mistress of the huge plantation.

Saunders came riding back up the road to the

Taylor mansion on the hill. He sat in the parlor, and held her hand, and offered his love again.

But no, she turned her head, tears streaking her cheeks. She still loved her dead husband.

Saunders walked out, down the porch steps, and mounted his horse for the lonely ride home.

Soon the guns of the Civil War boomed, and Saunders volunteered. He became a colonel in the Confederate Army and fought in the siege of Vicksburg. He was wounded while saving the life of a comrade, and lay near death in a hospital.

A carriage grated to a stop outside the hospital and Mary Taylor climbed down.

She walked into the hospital, found Saunders, and came to sit by his bed. She loved him, she said, and would marry him now.

She nursed him back to health, married him, and they lived out their lives near the banks of the Tombigbee, the Itomba Igaby, the box maker's creek, near the sunken, blackened hulk of the *Eliza Battle*.

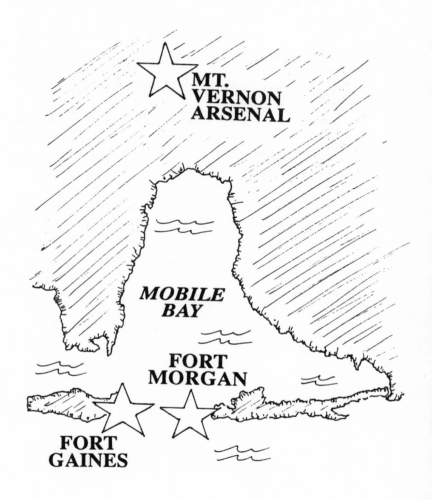

Chapter Seventeen

1861

Alabama militia Capture forts before Civil War begins

It was cold in the early light of Jan. 4, 1861, and the sunlight speckled the tops of the pine trees.

The U.S. Army soldiers, caretakers, slept on their cots inside the walled arsenal at Mt. Vernon, just north of Mobile, near the V where the Tombigbee flows into the Alabama River.

Nearby, in the arsenal warehouses, were stacks of guns and boxes of ammunition, all property of the U.S. Army.

There were noises at the edge of the pine woods, thumping sounds, like horses' hooves. And a low nickering sound, keen on the early morning air.

Horses? Deer? A soldier inside the wall may have stirred, listened drowsily, and pulled the Army issue blanket up over his shoulders. Probably just some animal out there.

In the nation's capital, far to the north in Washington, the winds of war were freshening. Abraham Lincoln had been elected president over his old enemy, Democrat Stephen Douglas, but Lincoln was home in Springfield, Ill. He would not be sworn into office until March of 1861,

Angry Southern Democrats, fuming that Douglas would not endorse slavery, had walked out of the Democratic convention and nominated Vice President John C. Breckenridge. This opened the way for Lincoln to win the election. Breckenridge ran a distant third, with the Southern vote and little else.

On Dec. 20, 1860, South Carolina pulled out of the Union, the first state to secede.

President James Buchanan, the lame duck sitting in the White House, would not leave office until March. Buchanan thought secession was illegal. But he also thought it was illegal for him to stop it. Impaled on the horns of this dilemma, he was immobilized as events whirled around him.

An anguished Lincoln, waiting for the mantle of the presidency to fall around his shoulders and hoping to keep his country from coming apart, sat in Springfield and watched, powerless to act.

But the impatient events would not wait for March, would not wait for Buchanan to pass the torch to Lincoln.

In Montgomery, Alabama Gov. Andrew Barry Moore—lawyer and judge from Marion, legislator from Perry County, former Speaker of the Alabama House of Representatives, sat in his office at the capitol and looked at a map.

He frowned, his strong forehead wrinkling the shock of white hair. He looked somewhat like another political Andrew, Old Hickory, Andrew Jackson of Tennessee.

On the map, he looked at the mouth of Mobile Bay and saw the potential trap. Two forts, Morgan on the eastern shore at Alabama Point, and the unfinished hulk of Fort Gaines on the eastern tip of Dauphin Island, seemed to reach to him like the pincers of a malignant military crab.

And north of Mobile, near the joining of the Tombigbee and the Alabama, lay the Mt. Vernon Arsenal, stocked to the rafters with guns and ammunition that Moore knew the Southerners would need if war came.

The forts and the arsenal were lightly garrisoned, Moore knew from intelligence reports. He winced, looking at the map. He was tempted. Why not take the forts now, before the Federals could rush in reinforcements? If they were reinforced, and war broke out, the two forts could cut off Mobile from the sea, and block one of the South's major ports.

The rumors came flitting, like snowflakes. The Federals had sent a fleet with reinforcements, the ships were standing off Mobile Bay even now. No, a battalion of U.S. Army troops were on forced march from somewhere, rushing to reinforce the forts by land.

Moore waited, and fingered the quill pen on his desk. Should he take the big chance? Take the forts, and risk war? Or leave them alone, and risk a stalemate at Mobile?

On Dec. 6, 1860, Moore had called for an Alabama election on Dec. 24. The election would choose delegates to a convention, which would begin Jan. 7 in Montgomery. The question before the convention: Should Alabama secede from the Union?

On Jan. 3, delegates were streaming into Montgomery, and the hotel lobbies were full of hot words, bitter words, words of secession and "cooperation," the code word for staying in the Union.

In the election, there were secessionists and cooperationists running for the delegate places. The secessionists barely got a majority.

On the Potomac in Washington, wily old Winfield Scott—hero of the Mexican War and commanding general of the U. S. Army, sat down to write a letter to the paralyzed Buchanan.

"From a knowledge of our Southern population...there is some danger of any early act of rashness preliminary to secession...the seizure of the some of the following posts..."

And the old man scribbled off the list of federal forts ringing the coast of the South—Ft. Jackson and Ft. Philip on the Mississippi; Ft. Morgan at Mobile; Pickens and McRee at Pensacola; Pulaski, below Savannah; Moultrie at Charleston, and Monroe, in Hampton Roads, across from Norfolk. He also listed Fort Sumter at Charleston.

All of them, Scott wrote, were dangerously open to capture because they had no garrisons, no soldiers, in any force. The forts were manned only by caretakers.

"In my opinion all these works should be immediately so garrisoned as to make any attempt to take any one of them, by surprise or *coup de main*, ridiculous."

Send more soldiers to the forts, quick before it's too late, he advised Buchanan.

But, as both Buchanan and Scott knew, the entire U.S. Army then numbered only 116,000 men, and many of these were chasing Indians in the West.

Buchanan read Scott's letter, and he saw the danger. But he could not act, he was paralyzed by indecision.

On Jan. 2 of the new year, with talk of secession sweeping the South, Governor Moore of Alabama looked at a new piece of paper on his desk, a telegram from

Joseph E. Brown, governor of Georgia.

Seize the two Alabama forts and the arsenal at Mt. Vernon, urged Governor Brown. Grab them *now*, before the federals can reinforce them.

A strange thing happened on Jan. 3 in Washington. An Alabama congressman, David Clopton, showed up at the War Department with a bold request and a straight face. He wanted "the plat and the plan of magazines at Mount Vernon Arsenal."

The War Department officials may have been shocked, but they weren't stupid. Clopton's request was summarily refused. Had Governor Moore asked Clopton to get information about the arsenal? History does not record the answer.

Sometime during the day of Jan. 3, Moore unrolled the map on his desk one more time, and looked at the ugly pincers which would choke the life out of Mobile if war came. Then he acted.

He wrote out a telegram, and a messenger took it down to the telegraph office. It was addressed to Col. J. B. Todd, commander of the First Volunteer Regiment at Mobile. These were Alabama state militia, not federal troops.

Organize your men, and all your movements must be in the greatest secrecy. Avoid bloodshed, but take Fort Morgan, Fort Gaines on Dauphin Island, and the Mt. Vernon arsenal. And take them now, quickly, without delay.

During the night of Jan. 3, the whispered word went out over Mobile. Soldiers of the regiment gathered at a secret place and moved out to the north, in the dark, toward the walled arson of Mt. Vernon.

As daylight peeped over the pine trees, there was a sudden movement in the woods, and the men of the First clambered over the walls of the arsenal, sweeping over the sleepy U.S. Army soldiers. They took the arsenal without firing a shot.

The men of the First Volunteer Regiment took an

inventory of everything in the arsenal, and gravely turned over a receipt to the fuming U.S. Army commander. He must have had some choice words for them, including treason.

The federal commander later reported to Washington that "this arsenal was taken possession by four companies of volunteers from Mobile at daylight this morning. I did not make, nor could I have made, any resistance, as they had scaled the walls and taken possession before I knew anything about the movement."

As yet, in early January of 1861, there was no Confederacy and no war. The firing on Fort Sumter would not come until April.

Governor Moore took his calculated risk, hoping that he would not begin the Civil War on Alabama soil. He bet that Buchanan would be frozen by indecision, and would not act. He was right.

Later in the day of Jan. 4, the volunteers marched into Fort Morgan, to find a single sergeant on duty. Again the militiamen gravely took an inventory, including a shot furnace to heat cannon balls before firing them, and solemnly gave the sergeant a receipt:

Received: one fort, brick.

Across the entrance to Mobile Bay, more Alabama militiamen walked into the still-unfinished Fort Gaines, and took it away from the few U.S. soldiers on duty.

In Montgomery, Governor Moore looked at the piece brought to him by an aide, and his face broke into a smile. It was a telegram from the Alabama commander in Mobile: The forts and the arsenal are ours, and there was no bloodshed. Moore watched for a response from President Buchanan, but there was none.

He smiled again. He had gotten away with it.

Moore sat down and dashed off a shrewd letter to President Buchanan. He told the president he had taken over the forts and the arsenal. Moore said he received information that Buchanan was planning to reinforce the forts and put a heavy guard on the arsenal.

"Having that information, it was but an act of self defense to take them," he said. And, prophetically, he wrote: "You must be sensible that no attempt at the coercion of the state, or at the enforcement by military power (by the U.S.) can be effectual, unless our utmost capacity for resistance can be exhausted."

It would have been a "suicidal" policy, Moore wrote, to allow the U.S. government to "enforce by war and bloodshed" a policy Alabama people would resist.

He told Buchanan that he took the forts and the arsenal to "avoid and not to provoke hostilities."

And so, on Jan. 4, 1861, three months before cannonballs whistled in the air over Fort Sumter in Charleston harbor to set off American's bloodiest war, Alabama militia captured three federal installations near Mobile.

The difference was Lincoln. When Moore took the forts at Mobile, Buchanan didn't have the nerve or inclination to object. When the Confederates fired on Sumter, Lincoln knew it meant war.

If there had been a pitched battle at Fort Morgan, or Fort Gaines, or Mt. Vernon, the war could have begun on Alabama soil..

For Fort Morgan and Fort Gaines, the time was to come, three years later, when Admiral David Farragut lay off Mobile with his federal fleet. Warned of mines in the bay, Farragut would damn the torpedoes (mines) and order full steam ahead. He stormed into the bay, took the forts back, took Mobile out of the war, and mortally wounded the Confederacy.

But, on Jan. 4, 1861, Governor Moore looked at his map, with the pincers blunted and tame, in his hands. Ahead for him lay secession, and service as a wartime governor in Alabama, and a dungeon in Fort Pulaski after the war, and bad health, and a quiet death at

Marion in 1873.

And, for the South, on that day, there lay ahead secession and blood and the guns of Sumter. Ahead were names like Manassas and the Wilderness and Chickamauga and Chancellorsville and Vicksburg and Shiloh.

And Gettysburg.

And Appomattox.

****

In the next volume of this series, you can watch Alabama, and Alabamians, caught in the terrible fire of the Civil War.

About the author

Clarke Stallworth grew up in Thomaston, a small town of 300 people in the Black Belt cotton region of South Alabama.

In his early teen years, Stallworth had two paper routes, one in the morning and one in the evening, so he became familiar with newspapers and the printed word early in life.

He tells of his "space ship," a green front porch swing at his home. He discovered books along with newspapers, and spent all his newspaper profits on books. With no library in town, he ordered a steady stream of books from mail-order publishers.

And in that front porch swing, as hundreds of loaded cotton wagons lined up to gin (the tiny town had three gins), he escaped the small town. With books, he could swim the Hellespont with Richard Halliburton, work alongside a coolie in a rice field with Pearl Buck, fight the Fascists in Spain with Ernest Hemingway.

He served as a seaman in the Navy during World War II, was called back in the Korean War and served as a lieutenant on a destroyer off Korea. He attended journalism school at the University of North Carolina, and came to Birmingham as a cub reporter on *The Birmingham Post* in 1948, covering the Ku Klux violence in 1949. At one point, a Klansman threw a hammer at his head, but missed.

As a reporter for *The Birmingham Post-Herald*, he covered the Phenix City cleanup by the Alabama National Guard and the Phenix City murder trials in 1954 and 1955. For his work in Phenix City, he was nominated for the Pulitzer Prize and won the Associated Press Sweepstakes for the best newspaper story in Alabama in 1954.

Beginning in 1956, he covered the Folsom, Patterson and Wallace administrations in the state capitol, and won AP newswriting prizes for eight straight years. He became city editor of *The Birmingham Post-Herald* in 1963, and directed the coverage of Birmingham's racial troubles. He served as managing editor of The *Columbus* (Ga.) *Ledger-Enquirer* in 1965 and 1966, returning to Birmingham to become city editor of *The Birmingham News*.

As city editor and managing editor of *The News*, he continued to write. He covered the opening day of the Vietnam talks in Paris in 1969, and wrote about the crushing defeat of freedom in Prague, as Russian tanks circled the city.

In 1979, he visited Cuba and wrote a series about life under the special brand of Cuban communism.

In 1980, he began a column called "Alabama Journey," wandering around the state, talking to interesting people. And he began a Sunday column of stories out of Alabama history, called "A Day in the Life of Alabama."

Stallworth retired from *The Birmingham News* in 1991, after 42 years in the newspaper business. He is now a writing consultant, doing workshops for newspaper reporters and editors. He has done more than 100 workshops for press associations in 40 states across the U.S. and Canada.

He has conducted 33 workshops for The American Press Institute in Reston, Va., and has taught journalism at the University of Alabama, Samford University, and the University of Alabama at Birmingham.

Stallworth is married to novelist Anne Nall Stallworth. Their daughter, Carole Stallworth Bennighof, is a music teacher in Birmingham, and their son, Clarke Stallworth III, is an art teacher at Ohio State University.